NEW POEMS
1973-74

THE P.E.N. ANTHOLOGIES
OF CONTEMPORARY POETRY

already published by Hutchinson of London

NEW POEMS 1960
Edited by Anthony Cronin, Jon Silkin, Terence Tiller
with a Foreword by Alan Pryce-Jones

NEW POEMS 1961
Edited by William Plomer, Anthony Thwaite, Hilary Corke
with an Introduction by the Editors

NEW POEMS 1962
Edited by Patricia Beer, Ted Hughes, Vernon Scannell
with an Introduction by the Editors

NEW POEMS 1963
Edited by Lawrence Durrell
with an Introduction by the Editor

NEW POEMS 1965
Edited by C. V. Wedgwood
with an Introduction by the Editor

NEW POEMS 1967
Edited by Harold Pinter, John Fuller, Peter Redgrove
with an Introduction by the Editors

NEW POEMS 1970–71
Edited by Alan Brownjohn, Seamus Heaney, Jon Stallworthy
with an Introduction by the Editors

NEW POEMS 1971–72
Edited by Peter Porter
with an Introduction by the Editor

NEW POEMS 1972–73
Edited by Douglas Dunn
with an Introduction by the Editor

The first seven P.E.N. anthologies were published
by Michael Joseph Limited

NEW POEMS

1973-74

A P.E.N. Anthology
of Contemporary Poetry

Edited by
STEWART CONN

HUTCHINSON OF LONDON

HUTCHINSON & CO (*Publishers*) LTD
3 Fitzroy Square, London W1

London   Melbourne   Sydney   Auckland
Wellington   Johannesburg   Cape Town
and agencies throughout the world

First published 1974
© P.E.N. 1974

Set in Monotype Ehrhardt
Printed in Great Britain by Benham and Company Limited,
Colchester, Essex, and bound by Wm Brendon,
Tiptree, Essex

ISBN 0 09 120400 3

ACKNOWLEDGEMENTS

Acknowledgement is gratefully made to the poets who have allowed their work to be included in this anthology, and to the following publishers and publications: *Agenda*; *Ambit*; *Anglo-Welsh Review*; *Antaeus*; *Aquarius*; *Edible Magazine*; *Encounter*; *Honest Ulsterman*; *Hudson Review*; *Irish Times*; *Lines*; *The Listener*; *Little Word Machine*; *London Magazine*; *Machars*; *New Statesman*; *Oasis*; *Observer*; *Oxford Poetry Magazine*; *Phoenix*; *Pink Peace*; *Planet*; *Poem of the Month*; *Poems '73*; *Poetry and Author*; *Poetry Book Society Christmas Supplement '73*; *Poetry Nation*; *Poetry Wales*; *Poni Press*; *Rainbow Press*; *Samphire*; *Scotsman*; *Scottish Poetry*; *Second Aeon*; *Stand*; *The Times Literary Supplement*; *Transatlantic Review*; *Triangle Press*; *Wave*; *Workshop*; and to the BBC.

Thanks are also due to Messrs Faber & Faber and to Messrs Jonathan Cape, for permission to include poems by W. H. Auden and William Plomer respectively.

*

New Poems 1973–74 is published with the assistance of the Arts Council of Great Britain.

CONTENTS

INTRODUCTION

The bulk of these poems have appeared in journals or magazines over the past twelvemonth; but none, to my knowledge, was due in hardback before this anthology went to press. I was also free to approach poets with whose work I was familiar. As a result, some as yet unpublished poems are included. My final selection was governed not only by the quality of each poem but by the balance of the volume as a whole. How, and of what, should (or could) it be representative?

*

A marked polarisation is evident in English poetry, and the public's response to it, today. One approach is that of the 'first thought, best thought' brigade. Another, drawing on folk lyrics, may be pleasing when sung but lacks any sense of discipline. Others include a colloquial, and a minimalist, school; a meticulous domestic verse; and, perhaps the extreme in retrenchment, an elegant brand of literary dandyism.

There are various responses to the basic dichotomy. One is that language should be 'lovingly explored as a medium, not rapidly marshalled to serve merely as expedient vehicle'. It is through using and adding to the resources of language that a poem succeeds; through its pattern of words and sounds, allied to sense, that it arrests the attention and captures the imagination.

This leaves ample room for interpretation. While I hope that editing *New Poems 1973–74* has nurtured my taste, there seems little point in acknowledging areas of activity or popularity at odds with my instinct and beliefs. A reassuring number of poets, fortunately, confirm that one of their functions is to create order from exper-ence—even the experience of chaos; and that poetry aiming at formal expression of thought and feeling need not lack immediacy or originality.

On the periphery, in particular, richly refined and diverse talen[t]
have emerged in recent years. Metropolitan publishers have com[e]
to look further and further afield for new names. The trend i[s]
healthy so long as it is for the right reasons, and provided th[e]
poetry's real strength underlies local colour.

This could have sociological implications. Two forces contrive t[o]
depersonalise our lives and those of the communities in which w[e]
live. One is the corruption of language; the debasing of our lingui[s]
tic heritage, through journalese and advertising. The other is th[e]
destruction of environment; the bureaucratic spoliation of th[e]
countryside and its replacement by concrete desert; the crushin[g]
uniformity of our cities.

The wilderness is where myth comes from: where imaginatio[n]
and metaphor, have their source. Destroy one, you imperil th[e]
other. The question is whether the poet responds to myth; wheth[er]
he is determined to 'purify the dialect of the tribe' and fight f[or]
what is under threat; and whether in the long run, and retainin[g]
contact with common speech, he (or she) is capable of doing so.

This does not preclude complementary developments, or pri[or]
pressures; any more for instance than the terms 'public' and 'pr[i]
vate' need be mutually exclusive. I suspect in any case that the be[st]
poetry will stem from a merging of disparate strains—as I think th[e]
best poems here do; and that the best poets will continue to appl[y]
intelligence and sensibility to experience, in such a way as to modi[fy]
that of their readers.

*

Having no hostages to fortune I was able to choose each poem f[or]
its own sake, because I liked it. Hospital visitors and young love[rs]
rub shoulders with a bog queen, John Donne, and an aspiring van[m]
pire. There are Shetland ponies, hares boxing, a dead fox, macab[re]
dogs. There are references to a gang slaying and to England[s]
exit from the World Cup. A lady loses her head; a boy flies a kite;

udge eats crow. There is a broad range of styles and commitments; a variety of energy and imagery; an air of poems that *demanded* to be written.

Certain poets I would have liked, but was unable, to include. Some, preparing collections, had nothing new to offer. Others proved hard to locate, or preferred to preserve silence. I must thank those poets and editors who responded so willingly, and who directed me to work I would otherwise have missed. My main concern, the vagaries of taste aside, still lies in the amount that may have passed me by. As it is, and whatever my sins of omission, I hope something of the exhilaration with which I came across so many of these poems will convey itself; and that the selection as a whole may give enjoyment.

Glasgow
November 1973

STEWART CONN

NEW POEMS 1973-74

Fleur Adcock

AN ILLUSTRATION TO DANTE

Here are Paolo and Francesca
whirled around in the circle of Hell
clipped serenely together
her dead face raised against his.
I can feel the pressure of his arms
like yours about me, locking.

They float in a sea of whitish blobs—
fire, is it? It could have been
hail, said Ruskin, but Rossetti
'didn't know how to do hail'.
Well, he could do tenderness.
My spine trickles with little white flames.

James Aitchison

LANDSCAPE WITH LAPWINGS

It's another April, and a day
with all the seasons in it, with lapwings
falling out of sunlight into rain,
stalling on a squall and then tumbling
over the collapsing wall of air
to float in zones of weightlessness again.

And on a day like this in such a place—
a few square miles of moorland in a round
of rounded hills, rain clouds and scattered trees,
with water flowing clearly over stone—
in such a place I feel the weights slip off
the way a lapwing would if it were me.

The place might form a frame of reference
for calculating weightlessness, or all
the weathers that are in one April day,
for drawing what conclusions can be drawn
from lapwings tumbling in and out of light
with such a total lack of gravity.

W. H. Auden

UNPREDICTABLE BUT PROVIDENTIAL

Spring with its thrusting leaves and jargling birds is here again
to remind me again of the first real Event, the first
genuine Accident, of that Once when, once a tiny
corner of the Cosmos had turned just indulgent enough
to give it a sporting chance, some Original Substance,
immortal and self-sufficient, knowing only the blind
collision experience, had the sheer audacity
to become irritable, a Self requiring a World
a Not-Self outside Itself, from which to renew Itself,
with a new freedom, to grow, a new necessity, death.
Henceforth, for the animate, to last was to mean to change,
existing both for one's own sake and that of all others,
forever in jeopardy.

              The ponderous ice-dragons
performed their slow-motion ballet, continents cracked in half
and wobbled drunkenly over the waters, Gondwana
smashed head-on into the under-belly of Asia,
but catastrophes only encouraged experiment.
As a rule it was the fittest who perished, the mis-fits,
forced by failure to emigrate to unsettled niches, who
altered their structure and prospered. (Our own shrew-ancestor
was a nobody, but still could take himself for granted,
with a poise our grandees will never acquire.)

                        Genetics
may explain shape, size and posture, but not why one physique
should be gifted to cogitate about cogitation,
divorcing Form from Matter, and fated to co-habit
on uneasy terms with its Image, dreading a double death,
a wisher, a maker of asymmetrical objects,
a linguist who is never at home in Nature's grammar.

Science, like Art, is fun, a playing with truths, and no game
should even pretend to slay the heavy-lidded riddle
What is the Good Life?

Common Sense warns me, of course, to buy
neither but, when I compare their rival myths of Being,
bewigged Descartes looks more outré than the painted wizard.

Eavan Boland

THE FAMINE ROAD

'Idle as trout in light Colonel Jones,
these Irish, give them no coins at all; their bones
need toil, their characters no less.' Trevelyan's
seal blooded the deal table. The Relief
committee deliberated: 'Might it be safe,
Colonel, to give them roads, roads to force
from nowhere, going nowhere of course?'

> *'one out of every ten and then
> another third of those again
> women—in a case like yours'*

Sick, directionless they worked; fork, stick
were iron years away; after all could
they not blood their knuckles on rock, suck
april hailstones for water and for food?
Why for that, cunning as housewives, each eyed—
as if at a corner butcher—the other's buttock.

> *'anything may have caused it, spores
> a childhood accident; one sees
> day after day these mysteries.'*

Dusk: they will work tomorrow without him.
They know it and walk clear; he has become
a typhoid pariah, his blood tainted, although
he shares it with some there. No more than snow
attends its own flakes where they settle
and melt, will they pray by his death-rattle.

> *'you never will, never you know
> but take it well woman, grow
> your garden, keep house, goodbye.'*

'It has gone better than we expected, Lord
Trevelyan, sedition, idleness, cured
in one; from parish to parish, field to field
the wretches work till they are quite worn
then fester by their work; we march the corn
to the ships in peace. This Tuesday I saw bones
out of my carriage window, your servant Jones.'

Barren, never to know the load
of his child in you, what is your body
now if not a famine road?

THE WAR HORSE

This dry night nothing unusual
About the clip, clop casual

Iron of his shoes as he stamps death
Like a mint on the innocent coinage of
earth.

I lift the curtain, watch the ambling feather
Of hock and fetlock, loosed from its daily
tether

In the tinker camp on the Enniskerry road
Pass, his breath hissing, his snuffling head

Down. He is gone. No great harm is done,
Only a leaf of our laurel hedge is torn.

Of distant interest like a bombed limb,
Only a rose which now will never climb

The stone of our house, expendable, a mere
Line of defence against him, a volunteer

You might say, only a crocus, its bulbous
head
Blown from growth, one of the screamless
dead.

But we, we are safe, our unformed fear
Of fierce commitment gone; why should we
care

If a rose, a hedge, a crocus are uprooted
Like corpses, remote, crushed, mutilated?

He stumbles on like a rumour of war, huge
Threatening; neighbours use the
subterfuge

Of blinds and curtains, he stumbles down
our street
Thankfully passing us; I pause, wait

Then to breathe relief lean on the sill
And for a second only my blood is still

With atavism: that rose he trampled stays
Ribboned across our hedge, recalling days

Of burned countryside, illicit braid—
A cause ruined before, a world betrayed.

Edwin Brock

FOX AT WINTERTON

All night the gale
had brought glass
wood and bodies
from the sea
using sand to make
a decent burial

leaving the beach
as ordered as
an Esher cemetery
each mound a mystery
except where a wing
or beak broke through
like weed.

I gave each one
a casual rite
dispensing death
like a clergyman
until I stopped
at a shape
as shocking as
a scream in church:

its red fur
stained the sand,
its head was chewed
into a fanged skull
and ten inches of rope
grew from its spine

yet enough of fox
remained to make
me flinch
expecting the massacre
to jump and snap and
infect my clean skin
with God knows what wounds

even walking away
I looked back
unless its stumps
stalked me along the beach:

not until another month
of tides had turned
it into tame bones
would I accept it.

This creature contained
so much life
its death shrieked,
shaming the quiet cough
that takes us
so barely alive
the air settles
where we were
without a sound.

George Mackay Brown

THE SHIP IN THE ICE

'The purpose of which voyage shall be: To discover a north-west
  passage by sea betwixt the oceans, for the furtherence of
  trade and the enhancement of her majesty's empire'. . . .

South-east wind, overcast, out of Gravesend. Bearing north,
  between dawn and the Longstone light.

The Forth. Two men committed to the courts for drunkenness.
  A seaman missing. Another taken from the stews.

Our mother the sea, receive us. Who bears, nourishes, chastises.
  The cold gray mother.

The Orkneys. A pilot: fierce whiskers, rum, pipe-spittle.
  Upthrust of Hoy, blue shoulders. Herring boats. Cair-
  ston, a wide bay. Hamnavoe and 38 howffs.

'Dear one, the only comfort I have in this bare place is to
  write to you and so I comfort myself and long for you.
  I carry your dear gift of linen in my sea-chest.'

The White Horse Inn. A whale-man turned away from our probings.

And north and west. Congregation of waters, a lamentation and
  a gossiping, unfathomed endless utterances, sisterhood of
  the sea. The North Atlantic.

The green heart of icebergs. Green and black undersea fires.
  The ice roared. Gray shuffling packs, the ice moved in
  behind us.

Here a man is as nature intended. Naked he goes among mirrors of
ice. Furled to the eyes, but naked, among prisms and
mirrors. He walks on a solid sea. Ice is everything.
A man eats ice.

Gentlemen, nothing remains for us, in these unfortunate
unlooked-for circumstances, but to leave the ship and
trek south. There are communities of Esquimeax all
down the coast. Take your guns and powder. Be of
good heart'. . .

Spalding died. Gregor can walk no further (leave him now.)
Trewick saw a piece of Cornwall in the snow: a spire,
rosebushes. We left Simpson to the bears. One knelt,
a flash in the hand, turned away: had white and red
stuff in his mouth afterwards.

Alone, on wrapped feet. Emerald, onyx, garnet burn. This
is an enchanted city. I go through the street of the
jewellers. A diamond blazes.

Wayne Brown

FACING THE SEA

1

My unextraordinary small-town girl
in flip-flops and a flimsy shift
and a sweater worn like a shawl,

you felt the cold come off the sea,
you squeezed your hands between your thighs,
you stared at the water. You said, 'Not me.
I done wid dis place. I goin' Kingston.'

And in Kingston once, in a sweat-wet bed,
a student nurse, whose name I've forgotten,
sat hugging a pillow, and finally said,
'I bored wid dis place. I goin' abroad.'

2

Pelicans

creaking on salt-crusted wings,
square-shouldered jets lumbering out, that
cigarette box on the rusty tide, this
frail flotsam of words: all things

travel endlessly outward.

I look at the water and cannot think
'Home is where we start from', or
'Reaching no absolute, in which to rest,
one is always nearer by not keeping still',

Until the woman starts up and points:

The floating city, that in ropes lay
blazing like iceberg the whole day,
is moving now, and though absently,

Like a hand lifted from memory
to sun-dried eyes, must, in its run,

blot warehouse, factory, market, hillside, sun. . .

Tom Buchan

GLASGOW SABBATH

Rum submerges
rain sheets off the hull heft of the Cuillin
ragged cattle
stand in their dunged pool at Elgol

and south by wet Mull
papercups half-buried in the beach at Dervaig
and the stunned Co-op van
with its turquoise sans serif motif

to the bubonic snatch of Glasgow
where volatile as monkeys
we die before our time
dazed with morphine in tiled wards

cloudcover sagging
a few stores open selling stale sliced bread
and coarse-faced couples
making for the coast

the streets littered
with hectic old women en route to vote for Christ
two or three late
croupiers and musicians in gaberdine

and a high-stepping paranoiac
agitating his metabolism in the dank park
where laurels drip and pale red
goldfish ruffle the milky mucus on their skins.

Charles Causley

TEN TYPES OF HOSPITAL VISITOR

1

The first enters wearing the neon armour
Of virtue.
Ceaselessly firing all-purpose smiles
At everyone present
She destroys hope
In the breasts of the sick,
Who realize instantly
That they are incapable of surmounting
Her ferocious goodwill.

Such courage she displays
In the face of human disaster!

Fortunately, she does not stay long.
After a speedy trip round the ward
In the manner of a nineteen-thirties destroyer
Showing the flag in the Mediterranean,
She returns home for a week
—With luck, longer—
Scorched by the heat of her own worthiness.

2

The second appears, a melancholy splurge
Of theological colours;
Taps heavily about like a healthy vulture
Distributing deep-frozen hope.

The patients gaze at him cautiously.
Most of them, as yet uncertain of the realities
Of heaven, hell-fire, or eternal emptiness,
Play for safety
By accepting his attentions
With just-concealed apathy,
Except one old man, who cries
With newly-sharpened hatred,
'Shove off! Shove off!
Shove. . . shove . . . shove . . . shove
Off!
Just you
Shove!'

3

The third skilfully deflates his weakly-smiling victim
By telling him
How the lobelias are doing,
How many kittens the cat had,
How the slate came off the scullery roof,
And how no-one has visited the patient for a fortnight
Because everybody
Had colds and feared to bring the jumpy germ
Into hospital.

The patient's eyes
Ice over. He is uninterested
In lobelias, the cat, the slate, the germ.
Flat on his back, drip-fed, his face
The shade of a newly dug-up Pharaoh,
Wearing his skeleton outside his skin,
Yet his wits as bright as a lighted candle,
He is concerned only with the here, the now,
And requires to speak
Of nothing but his present predicament.

It is not permitted.

4

The fourth attempts to cheer
His aged mother with light jokes
Menacing as shell-splinters.
'They'll soon have you jumping round
Like a gazelle,' he says.
'Playing in the football team.'
Quite undeterred by the sight of kilos
Of plaster, chains, lifting-gear,
A pair of lethally-designed crutches,
'You'll be leap-frogging soon,' he says.
'Swimming ten lengths of the baths'.

At these unlikely prophecies
The old lady stares fearfully
At her sick, sick offspring
Thinking he has lost his reason—

Which, alas, seems to be the case.

5

The fifth, a giant from the fields
With suit smelling of milk and hay,
Shifts uneasily from one bullock foot
To the other, as though to avoid
Settling permanently in the antiseptic landscape.
Occasionally he looses a scared glance
Sideways, as though fearful of what intimacy
He may blunder on, or that the walls
Might suddenly close in on him.

He carries flowers, held lightly in fingers
The size and shape of plantains,
Tenderly kisses his wife's cheek
—The brush of a child's lips—
Then balances, motionless, for thirty minutes
On the thin chair.

At the end of visiting-time
He emerges breathless,
Blinking with relief, into the safe light.

He does not appear to notice
The dusk.

6

The sixth visitor says little,
Breathes reassurance,
Smiles securely.
Carries no black passport of grapes
And visa of chocolate. Has a clutch
Of clean washing.

Unobtrusively stows it
In the locker; searches out more.
Talks quietly to the Sister
Out of sight, out of earshot, of the patient.
Arrives punctually as a tide.
Does not stay the whole hour.

Even when she has gone
The patient seems to sense her there:
An upholding
Presence.

7

The seventh visitor
Smells of bar-room after-shave.
Often finds his friend
Sound asleep: whether real or feigned
Is never determined.
He does not mind; prowls the ward
In search of second-class, lost-face patients
With no visitors
And who are pretending to doze
Or read paperbacks.

He probes relentlessly the nature
Of each complaint, and is swift with such
Dilutions of confidence as,
'Ah! You'll be worse
Before you're better.'

Five minutes before the bell punctuates
Visiting-time, his friend opens an alarm-clock eye.
The visitor checks his watch.
Market Day. *The Duck and Pheasant* will be still open.

Courage must be re-fuelled.

8

The eighth visitor looks infinitely
More decayed, ill and infirm than any patient.
His face is an expensive grey.
He peers about with antediluvian eyes
As though from the other end
Of time.
He appears to have risen from the grave
To make this appearance.
There is a whiff of white flowers about him;
The crumpled look of a slightly-used shroud.
Slowly he passes the patient
A bag of bullet-proof
Home-made biscuits,
A strong, death-dealing cake—
'To have with your tea',
Or a bowl of fruit so weighty
It threatens to break
His glass fingers.

The patient, encouraged beyond measure,
Thanks him with enthusiasm, not for
The oranges, the biscuits, the cake,
But for the healing sight
Of someone patently worse
Than himself. He rounds the crisis-corner;
Begins a recovery.

9

The ninth visitor is life.

10

The tenth visitor
Is not usually named.

Gillian Clarke

LUNCHTIME LECTURE

And this, from the second or third millenium
B.C., a female, aged about twenty-two.
A white, fine skull, full up with darkness
As a shell with sea, drowned in the centuries.
Small, perfect. The cranium would fit the palm
Of a man's hand. Some plague or violence
Destroyed her, and her whiteness lay safe in a shroud
Of silence, undisturbed, unrained-on, dark
For four thousand years. Till a tractor in summer
Biting its way through the longcairn for supplies
Of stone, broke open the grave and let a crowd of light
Stare in at her, and she stared quietly back.

As I look at her I feel none of the shock
The farmer felt as, unprepared, he found her.
Here in the Museum, like death in hospital,
Reasons are given, labels, causes, catalogues.
The smell of death is done. Left, only her bone
Purity, the light and shade beauty that her man
Was denied sight of, the perfect edge of the place
Where the pieces join, with no mistakes, like boundaries.

She's a tree in winter, stripped white on a black sky,
Leafless formality, brow, bough in fine relief.
I, at some other season, illustrate the tree
Fleshed, with woman's hair and colours and the rustling
Blood, the troubled mind that she has overthrown.
We stare at each other, dark into sightless
Dark, seeing only ourselves in the black pools,
Gulping the risen sea that booms in the shell.

Tony Connor

from THE MEMOIRS OF UNCLE HARRY

He invents a landscape to suit
various members of his family.

It is a landscape where high moor
collapses three hundred feet into pasturage.

The time is late evening when creeping darkness
settles and thickens endorsing solid forms.

His mother glares from behind an empty window
in a broken farm possessed by wind and weeds.

His children lie still in mid-air
before the limestone cliff they have slipped from.

His wife picks flowers beside a drained tarn.
With her tears she intends to replenish it.

He trudges up a road between dry stone walls
with nobody else in sight.
Birds fly out of the marshy grass,
but he does not see them.

At the lonely crossroads
where there was once a gallows
he forgets the wind for a moment.

His watch is at his ear.

The sky threatens a storm.

He wishes he could take all four roads.

He takes all four roads.

John Cotton

DOGS

Bluey—that rightly famed Australian dog
Waited his life out at the hospital
Where his swagman master had died.
Not knowing, Bluey hopefully eyed
All leavers for the return of a memory,
And we are filled with admiration
For such canine fidelity.
Yet there was another dog, Freud's chow
That cringed in a corner from the stench
Of his master's cancer. Can we allow
That dogs, too, prefer ideas to reality?

Kevin Crossley-Holland

RAPIDS

I

'Of course I will not go. I will be here.
Of course I'll still be here, I promise you.'
It is enough, I can still reassure
Them with words true now, not for tomorrow.
So they go off for conkers, shout, and fire
For unripe high-fliers; they break a bough. . .

What is there we do not wound with our touch?
My two sons, I cannot love you too much.

2

All afternoon he talked about that bridge
Through Salisbury, Stockbridge, Basingstoke and Staines.
The pressure of things we did not manage,
Tears suppressed, issues skirted like towns. . . .
We reached peeling London, parted, climbed, dodged
Pedestrians like unexploded mines,

Ran back towards each other. It was his cue.
'Can't you stay tonight? Please stay. Why must you . . .'

3

Don't keep asking. Let him open the door.
He is entitled to his privacy.
Isn't it enough for him to endure
This going, is it so necessary
To thrash it all out? No, he must first dare
Himself, the rapids of his misery.

This is a test of love. Leave him alone.
He is not mine, or hers; he is his own.

Donald Davie

MORNING

Rose late: the jarring and whining
Of the parked cars under my windows, their batteries drained,
Somehow was spared. When I let out our schoolboy
Into the street, it was good; the place was alive, and scented.

Spared too, for the most part, the puzzling tremulousness
That afflicts me often, these mornings. (I think
Either I need, so early, the day's first drink or
This is what a sense of sin amounts to:
Aghast incredulity at the continued success
Of my impersonation, the front put on to the world,
The responsibilities. . .)

Let all that go:
Better things throng these nondescript, barged-through streets
(The sun! The February sun, so happily far and hazy . . .)
Than a mill of ideas.

                    Sin, I will say, comes awake
With all the other energies, even at last the spark
Leaps on the sluggard battery, and one should have
Prosopopoeia everywhere: Stout Labour
Gets up with his pipe in his mouth or lighting
The day's first *Gaulois-filtre*; then stout
Caffein like a fierce masseur
Rams him abreast of the day; stout Sin
Is properly a-tremble; stout
Vociferous Electricity chokes and chokes,
Stumbles at last into coughings, and will soon
Come to the door with a telegram—'Operation
Some Day This Week'; and stout
Love gets up out of rumpled sheets and goes singing
Under his breath to the supermarket, the classroom,
The briskly unhooded
Bureaucratic typewriter. See how
Sol winks upon its clever keys, and Flora
In a northern winter, far underground,
Feels herself sore at nubs and nipples.

And that mob of ideas? Don't knock them. The sick pell-mell
Goes by the handsome Olympian name of Reason.

Peter Dent

THE ROOM

Your eyelids flicker
to sudden blades of light
that enter the room.

Party cars arriving late.

I watch your fingers
dip into a sheet
that puckers round your eyes.

You tease and press
and murmer to the voices you hear.

Rings glint
but you are the colour of linen.

Alan Dixon

THE SUNFLOWER COMPARED

The sunflower hangs its heavy head of seed
Like a wide standard-lamp that has gone out;
Its only enemy has been the wind;
Sun-like it shone that shame-faced dinner plate.
Eleven feet—too high for any room;
Its lower leaves, when withered, left their print;
Throughout its haughty progress I can claim
It stood assisted by my string and splint.
But now I snip the string and heave it up,
Its clotted root no bigger than the head
Which wildly wags without the help of wind:
A schizophrenic dumb-bell which I snap
To make an earth-mace and a pole-borne load
Like young mayoral hopes swung on the road.

Douglas Dunn

WHITE FIELDS

An aeroplane, its red and green night-lights
Spotting its distant noise in the darkness;
'Jack Frost', you say, pointing to white fields
Sparkling. My eyes accept the dark, the fields
Extend, spreading and drifting, fences rising
Before the black hedge that zips beside the road
I'm told I must never try to cross without you.
'What time is it?'—'The middle of the night!
You've had a dream, I heard you shout.'
It woke me and I cried aloud, until
My mother came and showed me the farm
Wasn't burning, the school still had its roof,
There was no one hidden in the little fir trees.
'Only an aeroplane!' As if you meant by that
That there in 1948 in Renfrewshire
We were safe from fear, and the white eyes
Of dead Jews were just photographs
In a terrible past, a neighbour's magazine.
'Only an aeroplane!' Unsleeping factories,
All night you busied overhead, and flames
Flushed out my cities made of shoe-boxes
And dominoes, my native village of shaws.
So innocent machine! I had a toy like you
That I made buzz and drone like Leaper's bees,
From which I dropped the A-bomb on John's pram,
Crumpling the hand-embroidered sheets.

Our breath melted ice on the window-pane.
Fields drizzled on the glass, opening strips
Of short-lived clarity, and fingernails of ice
Slid to the sill. 'No harm will come to us.'
I slept. Till now I've slept, dreaming of mice
Burrowing under the crusted tufts of snow
That heaviest fall had left us with,
Our planet flooded into continents
Of stray, white islands, a sea too cold to swim.
Till now I've slept, and waking, I reject
Your generation, an old copy of *Everybody's*
Thrown out with *Film Fun* and the tea-leaves,
Bulldozed by a conscript from our village
Into a pit dug by forced labour.
So easily is love shed, I hardly feel it.

White fields, your angled frost filed sharply
Bright over undisturbed grasses, do not soothe
As similes of innocence or idle deaths
That must happen anyway, an unmoral blankness;
Be unforgiving stillness, natural, what is:
Crimes uttered in landscape, smoke-darkened snow.

Trains in my distance altered. Cattle trucks
Seemed to chug through Georgetown, a station
Where a fat man in a black uniform kept hens
On the platform: but the waggons sprouted arms
And dropped dung, and no one sang
'Ten Green Bottles' or 'The Sash'. Offensive outings.

Six years old! And I lived through the worst of it!

THE COMPETITION

When I was ten, going to Hamilton
On the Leyland bus named for Eddlewood,
A boy with an aeroplane just like mine
Zoomed at his war games in the seat in front.
I'd never seen such a school uniform—
As brown as the manure in Cousar's coup
Where someone's city cousin had jumped in
Having been told it was 'just sand'—
One of Glasgow's best fee-paying places,
Brown as barrowloads from the blue-bottled byre.
I couldn't help it; I had to talk to him
And tell him I, too, had a Hurricane.
His mother pulled him to her, he sat sullen,
As if I'd spoiled his game. I spoke again,
And he called me a poor boy, who should shut up.
I'd never thought of it like that.
The summer tenements were so dry I cried.
My grandfather wouldn't give him sixpence.

Years later, running in a race, barefooted
As I'd trained my spikes to ruin, convinced
My best competitor was him, I ran into
The worst weathers of pain, determined to win,
But on the last lap, inches from the tape, was beaten
By someone from Shotts, Miners Welfare Harriers Club.

D. J. Enright

VACILLATIONS OF AN ASPIRING VAMPIRE

'Guaranteed and proven', said Rousseau,
A man of reason. 'The evidence is complete.'

I shall wear two fine pointed teeth
And a charming manner.
The ladies will be dressed in décolletage.
Nothing's more taking than necks and breasts.
The tooth is nearer to the nerve-centre,
The mouth is nearer to the heart.
This is the height of intimacy,
The rest is low and brutish.

It means a lot, when all your life
You've lacked both power and charm.
The tonics they gave me as a child
Did nothing for the blood.
My teeth are made of chalk.
I was weaned too early.
I have had trouble with bras.

'The testimony of persons of quality',
Said Rousseau. 'Surgeons, priests and judges.'

But the laws require a tooth for a tooth.
I must be hospitable to strangers,
I shall have to give up garlic
And hide away the rood that came from Lourdes.
For first I too must die beneath the charmer's lips.

And even then, how short-lived
Immortality can be!
I see a cross nestling between full breasts,
I see myself unseen in a mirror,
I see a policeman bearing a pointed stake.

I fear those persons of quality,
Those surgeons, priests and judges,
And the patrons of cinemas.
You could lose what little blood you have.

Gavin Ewart

WILLIAM McGONAGALL ON ENGLAND'S FAILURE TO QUALIFY FOR THE WORLD CUP, 1974

Now that the English have discovered they're on a sticky
wicket
And their Test teams aren't as good as they thought they
were at cricket,
And they've now absolutely completely lost face
Even at football, what will the Nation do about this
disgrace?
I think they ought all to swarm to the cliffs and in
communal despair
Throw themselves into the sea, in a noble mass suicide
darkening the air.

Roy Fisher

COMMUTER

Shallow, dangerous, but without sensation:
sun beats in the rear view mirror
with cars squatting in the glare
and coming on. This continues.
Gasholders flicker along the horizon.

Out in all weathers on the test rig
that simulates distance by substituting
a noise drawn between two points;
shallow, my face printed on the windscreen,
profile on the side glass; shallow—

Either I have no secrets
or the whole thing's a secret
I've forgotten to tell myself:
something to make time for on the night run south,
when the dazzle turns to clear black
and I can stare out over the wheel
straight at Orion, printed on the windscreen.

A GRAMMAR FOR DOCTRINE

Not what
neutralizes by balance
or by extension
cancels—

This is the cleft:
rate it how you will,
as an incredible thing
with tangible properties
even. But without doubt
the thing that is
shown to people.

Real emphasis
only in the plainness of the signs
for what's known;

mystification itself,
eternal sport,
opens a coloured arch,
plastic to the core,

and a tram with little decoration

sends courageous Gaudi to Avernus.
Entry is quick, you never sense it,
return by way of what's known:
entry is quick, you never sense it,
however you repeat it, or hang by a hair.

Roger Garfitt

THE HITCH-HIKER

One hand crabs along the seat back,
prising a grip; one sensory foot
hovers down, testing the floor,
testing the temperature. He hangs
over the seat, as over a piping bath,
inching himself down.

There's a knife-edge brim on his old felt,
his muffler ties as neatly as silk:
of his natty dress, only the skills remain.
Nothing else's quite right: a hold-all for shopping,
trousers fraying at the knee. Old vanities
are the best he can do.

Alone at a bus stop, on the verge of the by-pass:
these are the Home Counties of the Moon. The present
starves him in its thin atmosphere. Death
is coming over him like a yawn.
He hitched a lift, his admission of exile
a shy elocution of the thumb.

He's talked himself down to the seat.
He muffs the door shut. I edge into gear
as he perches there, all nerves and bone.
He leans back, and identity rises in him
—he's got his second wind. He remarks,
'You're nowhere without a car these days,
are you?'

HARES BOXING

This way and that
goes the runaway furrow.
Nose to tail
goes the tunnel
in the grass.

Now the leader
swivels, jerks up his heels.
The trick flickers
along the rope of hares:
heels over head they go, head over heels.

It's the Saturday
after Valentine:
in Florey's Stores
the kids go
into huddles.

Ooh! What did he put?
Go on, tell us! we *promise*
we won't tell.

Did she send you one?
    Did she?

Over the winter nothing has changed
but the land. The hedgerows
are in heaps for burning.
The owl's tree stands vacant
between the scars of smooth earth.

The sunlight falls on distances,
on the old lines. The hares meet
as they met before Enclosure, far out
in the drift of grasses, their fisticuffs
like tricks of the eye.

What catches the light, what the eye believes
is the rufous shoulder, the chest's white blaze:
what it sees are up on their haunches
the blaze throw its guard up, the shoulder
slide in a punch: two pugs that dual

stripped to the waist by sunlight.
And the Fancy? They emerge
from the corners of the eye, low company
from the lie of the land, with guineas
in their stare, without visible means.

The purse is all he fancies. The generations
bunch in his arm.
Toora-li-ooral go the fifes in his blood.
As tall, as straight as a thistle,
Jack Hare squares up to Dancing Jack.

Raymond Garlick

THE POETRY OF MOTION

To see the Moscow-bound express withdraw
from Amsterdam; imperial, remote,
intent as a risen tsar returning
incognito. The destination boards,
in Latin and Cyrillic scripts, intone
a litany of cities: brown Berlin,
white Warsaw, and magnificent below
the dawns of three days' journeying, Moscow.

I once went to Italy
the whole way by wagon-lit,
Arnhem–Milan, on the Rome
express: its cabin a home
from home, inviolate cell
on that serpentine hotel
gliding through Europe. No one
but the steward and the sun
disturbed me for two whole days.
Washed by seas of light and haze
Germany and Switzerland
unfolded, flowed, to be scanned
by the wide picture-window—
whose flashing mirror, or glow
at sunset, signalled them peace,
wonder, and a heart at ease.

And then the Hoek, when the night-boat
slides in at dawn, and all those great
expresses stand—the *Lorelei*,
the *Scandinavie* and the rest,
like horizontal rockets poised
for count-down, lift-off, flawless launch;
waiting for some arch-guard to fire
the touchpaper and then retire
immediately as off we flare.
I think too of a tired express
that campaigned all day round Navarre
and Aragon and Old Castile
until, like an exhausted Cid,
at last it stumbled on Madrid.

But it's the old *Welshman* that I recall
from that steaming railway age best of all—
mid-morning train from antique Euston's drear
Abandon-hope-all-ye-who-enter-here
style of décor. Luncheon served about Crewe—
by the discobolus waiter who threw
in perfect parabola a full plate
of consommé when the train, a little late,
moved injudiciously. And after
these delights, Mr Hughes Stationmaster
in rosebud, neatly furled, and yachting cap
waiting to welcome you (against the lap
of sea on the down platform) in the sails
of his regatta'd speech, home to Wales.

Valerie Gillies

FELLOW PASSENGER

Mister B. Rajan, diamond buyer,
crystallises from this travelling companion.
He goes by rail, it seems, by criss
and by cross, Hyderabad to Bangalore
to Madras, Madras, Madras,
seeking the industrial diamond.

He brings new orient gems from hiding.
Himself, he wears goldwealthy rings
of ruby, and, for fortune,
another of God Venkateśwaren.
His smile is a drillpoint diamond's,
incisive his kindness.

Sparrowboned, he walks unstable passageways,
living on boiled eggs and lady's-fingers
with noggins of whisky to follow.
He dreams of his house, the shrineroom picture
of Sai Baba, corkscrew-haired young saint.
And he has at home beautiful hidden daughters.

Henry Graham

AN AFTERNOON AT LA GRANDE JATTE

The retired jockey ignores the monkey
while the dog with the ribbon
becomes a pig, before
my very eyes. Madam has taken
her monkey for its usual walk.
Monsieur has come to watch
his mistress fish for letters
in this very french river. Even
the stranded trombone player
playing the Marseillaise to the two
tin soldiers is in love
with everything. Stravinsky died today.

I listen to Pulcinella and take
another drink as all
these very french people
hold their breath and stand
very still in sorrow
in the sun.

I think I see between the trees
and the spots before my very eyes, caused
by the ruin of my liver, Igor
standing with a parasol.

I think the fire bird has
flown into the sun forever.

Thom Gunn

DIAGRAMS

Downtown, an office tower is going up.
And from the mesa of unfinished top
Big cranes jut, spectral points of stiffened net:
Angled top-heavy artefacts, and yet
Diagrams from the sky, as if its air
Could drop lines, snip them off, and leave them there.

On girders round them, Indians pad like cats,
With wrenches in their pockets and hard hats.

They wear their yellow boots like moccasins,
Balanced where air ends and where steel begins,
Sky men, and through the sole's flesh, chewed and pliant,
They feel the studded bone-edge of the giant.
It grunts and sways through its whole metal length.
And giving to the air is sign of strength.

BABY SONG

From the private ease of Mother's womb
I fall into the lighted room.

Why don't they simply put me back
Where it is warm and wet and black?

But one thing follows on another.
Things were different inside Mother.

Padded and jolly I would ride
The perfect comfort of her inside.

They tuck me in a rustling bed
—I lie there, raging, small, and red.

I may sleep soon, I may forget,
But I won't forget that I regret.

A rain of blood poured round her womb,
But all time roars outside this room.

Michael Hamburger

NEWSPAPER STORY

Santa Barbara News Press
Feb. 16th, 1973

1

In Hartford City, Indiana,
Lived a factory worker, Gary,
Patriotic enough to invest
What little cash he could spare
In US Savings Bonds.
His reward came in the shape
Of a flag. But not rich enough
To own a house, an apartment
Or a flagpole on which to hang it,
Gary pinned up the flag
In his minibus as a curtain.

2

When Gary was arrested
For desecrating the flag
His hair was noted to be
Of un-American length;
And the minibus, too, his home,
Was not of American make.

3

Just when the Vietnam heroes
Were due for repatriation
Gary was sentenced to bear
Old Glory for three hours
Outside the City Hall.
While police guards stood by
He was watched by a mixed crowd
Of longhairs, Boy Scouts
And American Legionnaires
In full regalia. The word
'Commie' was shouted repeatedly.

4

Gary might have been fined.
But the judge, a patriot too,
Thought public penance more apt.
'The intent was embarrassment',
He commented later. 'A fine
Wouldn't reach that man.'

5

'What could I do?' asked Gary.
'I ain't got 1000 dollars.
It wasn't much of a choice.
Either look like an idiot,
Slapped in the stocks, jeered at
As a communist or something,
Or else let my wife and kids
Go hungry.'

6

          Strange, in the end
Everyone seemed to weaken.
Gary after one hour
Withdrew to the courtroom, to finish
His penance beneath a plaque
Bearing the pledge of allegiance,
And so made the penance private—
Not, to be sure, because
Of the biting winter winds.
The publicity hurt his credit,
His father's, too, and his wife's.
Indeed he demanded review
Of his case in a Circuit Court.

The judge said: 'Being a veteran,
Proud of my country and flag,
I'd probably do it again.'

Probably? There was the chink
Where the rot of treason sets in.
That judge was eating crow.

TWO PHOTOGRAPHS

I

At an outdoor table of the Café Heck
In the Munich Hofgarten
Six gentlemen in suits
And stiff white collars
Are sitting over coffee
Earnestly talking.
The one with a half-moustache
Wears a trilby hat.
The others have hung up theirs,
With their overcoats, on hooks
Clamped to a tree.
The season looks like spring.
The year could be '26.

On a hook otherwise bare
Hangs a dogwhip.

No dog appears in the picture—

An ordinary scene.
Of all the clients
At adjoining tables
None bothers to stare.

2

The year is '33.
The gentleman in a trilby
Is about to board a train.
Behind him stand
Four men in black uniforms.
'For his personal protection'
The Chancellor of the Reich
Carries a dogwhip.

No dog appears in the picture.

Seamus Heaney

ACT OF UNION

1

Tonight, a first movement, a pulse,
As if the rain in bogland gathered head
To slip and flood—a bog-burst,
A gash breaking open the ferny bed.
Your back is a firm line of eastern coast
And arms and legs are thrown
Beyond your gradual hills. I caress
The heaving province where our past has grown.
I am the tall kingdom over your shoulder
That you would neither cajole nor ignore.
Conquest is a lie. I grow older
Conceding your half-independent shore
Within whose borders now my legacy
Culminates inexorably.

2

And I am still imperially
Male, I am leaving you with your pain:
The rending process in the colony,
The battering ram, the boom burst from within.
The act sprouted an obstinate fifth column
Whose stance is growing unilateral.
His heart beneath your heart is a wardrum
Mustering force. His parasitical
And ignorant little fists already
Beat at your borders and I know they're cocked
At me across the water. No treaty
I foresee will salve completely
Your tracked and stretchmarked body, the big pain
That leaves you raw, like opened ground, again.

BONE DREAMS

1

White bone found
on the grazing:
the rough, porous
language of touch

and its yellowing, veined
impression in the grass,
like an opened pod.
As dead as stone,

flint-find, nugget
of chalk,
I touch it again,
I wind it in

the sling of mind
to pitch it
and follow its
drop into speech.

2

Bone-house:
a skeleton
in the tongue's
old dungeons.

I push back
through dictions,
Elizabethan foliage,
Norman devices,

the erotic mayflowers
of Provence
and the ivied latins
of churchmen

to the scop's
twang, the iron
flash of consonants
cleaving the line.

3

In the coffered
riches of grammar
and declensions
I found *bān-hūs*,

its fire, benches,
wattle and rafters:
where the soul
fluttered a while

in the roof-space.
There was a small pot
for the brain
and a cauldron

of generation
swung at the centre—
love-den, blood-holt,
bone-hoard, dream-bower.

4

Come back past
philology and kennings,
re-enter memory
where the bone's lair

is a love-nest
in the grass.
I hold my lady's head
like a crystal

and ossify myself
by gazing: I am screes
on her escarpments,
a chalk giant

carved upon her downs.
Soon my hands on the sunken
fosse of her spine
move towards the passes.

BOG QUEEN

I lay waiting
between turf-face and demesne wall,
between heathery levels
and glass-toothed stone.

My body was braille
for the creeping influences:
dawn suns groped over my head
and cooled at my feet,

through my fabrics and skins
the seeps of winter
digested me,
the illiterate roots

pondered and died
in the cavings
of stomach and sockets.
I lay waiting

on the gravel bottom,
my brain darkening,
a jar of bog-spawn
fermenting underground

dreams of Baltic amber.
Bruised berries under my nails,
the vital hoard reducing
in the crock of the pelvis.

My diadem grew carious,
gemstones dropped
in the peat floe
like bearings of history.

My sash was a black glacier
wrinkling, dyed weaves
and phoenician stitchwork
retted on my breasts'

soft moraines.
I knew winter cold
like the nuzzle of fjords
at my thighs—

the soaked fledge,
the swaddle of hides.
My skull hibernated
in the wet nest of my hair.

Which they robbed.
I was barbered
and stripped
by a turfcutter's spade

who veiled me again
and packed the coomb
softly between stone jambs
at my head and my feet.

Till a peer's wife bribed him.
The plait of my hair,
a slimy birth-cord
of bog, had been cut

and I rose from the dark,
hacked bone, skull-ware,
frayed stitches, tufts,
small gleams on the bank.

Lois March Herrickson

HOME

In a house hissing with cruelty
I came across a child cheerful and lively
Sitting under sick gusts of anger and agony
Like a little tinker under a lip of ironsheet
When the day downpours. 'Well then' I cried, 'tell me
Why your face is scatheless, why no burns
Blister your arms, and your ribs are invisible?'
And the child, with a smile of godly self-gratulation—
'I am my mammy's only good bairn.'

GANG SLAYING ANNIVERSARY

As the driftwood slaps upchannel and the wind hooks water
A woman stands by the Thames, and no-one else,
Nobody else to hear her cries:
'Arise, Ginger Marks, O my love,
O rise, my love, my Ginger Marks, arise.'

David Holbrook

THE KITE

It leaps, out of his hands,
And takes its place in the air, at once.
It hangs, steady, above the fair child
Who dances under it, stretching up his arms.

We have gone straight to our goal:
As the showers dashed their last
Drenchings into the shivering primroses,
Leaving behind pale sun and a wind
Tom and I tacked in a new splint,
Made for the highest hill, up on the Moor.

People sit in their cars, reading the papers:
Some children chip at rocks with hammers.
Lovers hold hands and skip: another kite
Circulates crazily in an eddy, crashes.

We tug our same string gently, pay
All we have left out from the reel.
No world but the slip of wood, the string,
The receding coloured stuff on its brittle frame.

'It will go right up to the sky.' The clouds
Are high in the sunlight. I feel their wreathes.
Am swallowed in them, as I used to be
As a child: Tom's kite draws me
Floating above Haytor, lost in the air.

We add a ball of red twine, hand
By hand, until, far bird in the light,
The kite is in the steady gale up there,
And we walk tugging it up to the rocks.

We sit under a shelf, sublimely happy.
Tom looks at me; the pleasedness on his face
Shining in every freckle. The kite
Begins to talk to us—a high whistle
Set up in the string, and thrilling in the reel.
Our realm is up there, in the high pure wind:
We fly about, like two blent essences.

A good wind-down, mundane return:
Anxieties foregather: we have tea.

But Tom and I still hold our string,
And feel the vibrating heart that exists only
So long as there is wind—and know how free
The mind, fixed in single attention so, can be!

Glyn Hughes

LABOR OMNIA VINCIT

A senile townscape has its heart cut out
for a fresh disfiguring. 'The new
by-pass will, after all, go through
the town centre.'

The minarets of a tilting cinema—
one foundation sunk in the rubbery river
that doesn't grant that lightening of the heart
expected of water—

will make a fine, sclerosis dust
when the new rovers, craftsmen's sons,
tear it down for motherly icons
of the mythic North to clean from their furniture.

As I scavenge the sites and the vast dustbins
they've made of the quarries whence it came, for stone
lintels to restore my home, I recognise
a drunken recklessness in their dusty eyes.

Ted Hughes

(from a cycle of poems for children on The Seasons)
NEW YEAR SONG

Now there comes
    The Christmas rose
      But that is eerie
              too like a ghost
      Too like a creature
              preserved under glass
      A blind white fish
              from an underground lake
      Too like last year's widow
                  at a window
         And the worst cold's to come.

Now there comes
    The tight-vest lamb
      With its wriggle eel tail
              and its wintry eye
      With its ice-age mammoth
                unconcern
      Letting the aeon
              seconds go by
      With its little peg hooves
               to dot the snow
      Following its mother
              into worse cold and worse
         And the worst cold's to come.

Now there comes
    The weak-neck snowdrops
      Bouncing like fountains
                    and they stop you, they make you
        Take a deep breath
                    make your heart shake you
        Such a too much of a gift
                    for such a meantime
        Nobody knows
                    how to accept them
        All you can do
                    is gaze at them baffled
              And the worst cold's to come.

And now there comes
    The brittle crocus
      To be nibbled by the starving hares
                    to be broken by the snow
        Now comes the aconite
                    purpled by cold
        Now comes a song
                    into the storm-cock's fancy
        And the robin and the wren
                    they rejoice like each other
        In an hour of sunlight
                    for something important
              Though the worst cold's to come.

THE WARM AND THE COLD

Freezing dusk is closing
   Like a slow trap of steel
On trees and roads and hills and all
   That can no longer feel.
      But the carp is in its depth
         Like a planet in its heaven.
      And the badger in its bedding
         Like a loaf in the oven
      And the butterfly in its mummy
         Like a viol in its case
      And the owl in its feathers
         Like a doll in its lace.

Freezing dusk has tightened
   Like a nut screwed tight
On the starry aeroplane
   Of the hurtling night.
      But the trout is in its hole
         Like a giggle on a sleeper.
      The hare strays down the highway
         Like a root going deeper.
      The snail is dry in the outhouse
         Like a seed in a sunflower.
      The owl is pale on the gatepost
         Like a clock on its tower.

Moonlight freezes the shaggy world
　　Like a mammoth of ice—
The past and the future
　　Are the jaws of a steel vice.
　　　　But the cod is in the tide-rip
　　　　　Like a key in a purse.
　　　　The deer are on the bare-blown hill
　　　　　Like smiles on a nurse.
　　　　The flies are behind the plaster
　　　　　Like the lost score of a jig.
　　　　Sparrows are in the ivy-clump
　　　　　Like money in a pig.

Such a frost
　　The freezing moon
　　　Has lost her wits.

　　　　A star falls.

The sweating farmers
　　Turn in their sleep
　　　Like oxen on spits.

PROMETHEUS ON HIS CRAG

(from a longer sequence with the same title)

His mother covers her eyes.
The mountain splits its sweetness.
The blue fig splits its magma.

Birth-hacked flesh-ripeness.
The cry bulging, a slow mire
Bubbles scalded.

The mountain utters
Blood and again blood.
Puddled, blotched newsprint.

Crocus evangels.
A mountain is flowering
A gleaming man.

Cloud-bird
Midwifes the upglare naphtha,
Opening the shell.

As Prometheus eases free
And sways to stature
And balances, and treads

On the dusty peacock film where the world floats.

Elizabeth Jennings

GROWING

Not to be passive simply, never that.
Watchful, yes, but wondering. It seems
Strange, your world, and must do always, yet
Haven't you often been caught out in dreams

And changed your terms of reference, escaped
From the long rummaging with words, with things,
Then found the very purpose that you mapped
Has moved? The poem leaves you and it sings.

And you have changed. Your whispered world is not
Yours any longer. It's not there you grow.
I tell you that your flowers will find no plot

Except when you have left them free and slow,
While you attend to other things. Do not
Tamper with touching. Others pick, you know.

George Kendrick

PHOBIA

1

None of their kind can be killed with the dictionary.
When the brains are out, the legs necromance
after their persecutors and their helpers.
Miles out at sea they track you, parachutists
on a gossamer. Two million to the acre
they populate even the sands and shallows,
ambush the slow bird, hollow the living
bee into a plastercast of his own
terror. Trees are crazy with them. Every house
has its ten thousand squatting behind walls,
locked in the attic: their myth is our mad cousin,
who adapts in the mind, and is more various
than all its vanities and scheming cells.

2

In camp, they spoke of one in the signal office
that pattered around the table like a mouse
—until somebody slammed it with the Log.
Before they could move to decode his scrambled limbs
the book jerked upward like the stone of a tomb;
a tawny shadow sped into a hole.

More feared than scorpions, we heard on arrival.
A double-jointed knuckle in the jaw
cramps them to flesh. They have to be torn or
cut away from you, leaving a scar.
A man went screaming berserk at Deversoir
with one cleated insanely below his eye.

3

Hermit or saint might end up loving spiders,
camels with green teeth, shit-beetles—
reality, for all its stench and venom.
Nineteen, you lie awake at night. Mosquitoes
embroider the net, voices like shooting stars.
The calendar crawls through your nights of service.

Thomas Kinsella

38 PHOENIX STREET

Look.
       I was lifted up
past rotten bricks weeds
to look over the wall.
A mammy lifted up a baby on the other side.
Dusty smells. Cat. Flower bells
hanging down purple red.

Look.
        The other. Looking
My finger picked at a bit of dirt
on top of the wall and a quick
wiry redgolden thing
ran back down a little hole.

*

We knelt up on our chairs in the lamplight
and leaned on the brown plush, watching the gramophone.
The turning record shone and hissed
under the needle, liftfalling, liftfalling.
John McCormack chattered in his box.

Two little tongues of flame burned
in the lamp chimney, wavering
their tips. On the glassy belly
little drawnout images quivered.
Jimmy's mammy was drying the delph in the shadows.

*

Mister Cummins always hunched down
sad and still beside the stove,
with his face turned away toward the bars.
His mouth so calm, and always set so sadly.
A black rubbery scar stuck on his white forehead.
Sealed in his sad cave. Hisshorror erecting
slowly out of its rock nests, nosing the air.
He was buried for three days under a hill of dead,
the faces congested down all round him
grinning *Dardanelles!* in the dark.
They noticed him by a thread of blood
glistening among the black crusts on his forehead.
His heart gathered all its weakness, to beat.

A worm hanging down, its little round
black mouth open. Sad father.

*

I spent the night there once
in a strange room, tucked in against the wallpaper
on the other side of our own bedroom wall.

Up in a corner of the darkness the Sacred Heart
leaned down in his long clothes over a red oil lamp
with his women's black hair and his eyes lit up in red,
hurt and blaming. He held out the Heart
with his women's fingers, like a toy.

The lamp–wick, with a tiny head
of red fire, wriggled in its pool.
The shadows flickered: the Heart beat!

George MacBeth

3

Tonight the poet is reading. He stands on wood
  in a bare hall. Before him
  some twenty or thirty young women
hunch over their desks and glower. The poet is something
  new. They have come to listen.
  They all, in their own way, write
and the poet, in his way, will show them how the professional
writes. A harsh overhead light glares. One shifts

with a hiss of tights. The poet observes, as he reads,
  a distracting world of thighs
  he would like to stroke. In his mind
he strokes the thighs. The young women, as women are,
  aware of his looking, reveal
  rather more than before. He reads
in a dubious mist of lust. Meanwhile, the mistress
glints through her spectacles, and is bright as a bird.

She is neither a bird nor a mistress. The room is cold
  and the poet heats his feet
  with a soft-shoe shuffle across
the barren boards. A girl titters. Her breasts
  under her wool sweater
  heave and invite. Encouraged,
the poet attempts a more comical poem. In his mind
an image of after the reading emerges. He strokes it.

Well, are you ready for questions? The spectacles glint
    as the plain ones parade their minds
    with a show of force. With a sigh
the poet sinks back. He deals with the questions. He gives
    what they need. He is charming and kind.
    He feels old. As the evening ends
with the usual round of applause, the poet retires,
refusing cocoa. He walks to his car in the rain.

10

The Poet is buying a cat. The cats glare
    from behind the tight wire
    which protects the poet from them. He
pokes his finger, gingerly, into one's ginger
    fur. It stirs, with a growl,
    like a dog. The poet withdraws,
uneasily nursing himself. He walks on to the purr
of a grey dollop of elephant-coloured ice-cream

flounced on a blanket. Frowning, it stares at the poet
    as if he has just been emptied
    out of a tin. It doesn't
want to eat him. The poet attunes himself
    to the feline mood. He moves
    from cage to cage, growling
and frowning. He growls and frowns like a cat. *Can I
help you?* A face, the first he has seen with a smile,

blocks his advance. The poet adjusts his growl
    to a cough. *No, thank you, I need
    something a little smaller.*
He needs a small cat. He would like a small, friendly cat.
    There are no small friendly cats.
    All purr, and are fierce. The poet
despairs of buying a cat. He edges towards
the Emergency exit. Outside, a chained dog howls.

Norman MacCaig

BIRTHDAYS

In the earliest light of a long day
three stags stepped out from the birch wood
at Achmelvich bridge
to graze on the sweet grass
by the burn.
A gentle apparition.

Stone by stone a dam was built,
a small dam, small stone by stone.
And the water backed up, flooding
that small field.

I'll never see it again.
It's drowned forever.
But still
in the latest light of a lucky day I see
horned heads come from the thickets
and three gentle beasts innocently pacing
by that implacable water.

FOR A BIRTHDAY CARD

A bird sang from an ivy spray
'Elaine is twenty-one today.'
I took it by the throat and cried
'You ruffianly wee bird, you lied,
Or you'd bewail her sweet-and-twenty,
Larghetto e dolentamente.

He coughed a bit, then said to me
(Vivace ma cantabile)
'If there's one thing you ought to know
Time licks along prestissimo
And though she's not as old as Pharaoh
She's growing (dolce e leggiero).'

Con spirito I answered, 'Plenty
Need to talk so largamente
When she is wrinkled, bent and hoary.
So modulate from your minore—
Sing (though your voice is only so-so)
How she is dolce a grazioso.'

The bird got tough as Marlon Brando
And chirped right back at me, sforzando,
'Baloney from a phoney crony
Though uttered con espressione
Will introduce no ritardando
In Time's sempre accelerando.'

I sighed and said, 'I know it's best to
Admit Time's natural tempo's presto,
And we go through our short libretto
Never slower than allegretto.
She lives con brio; but sense tells you to
See she lives also sostenuto.'

He (pizzicato) clapped his beak
And said, 'It's good to hear you speak
So affetuoso and vivace.
I'll sing as soppy as Liberace
And praise her till I'm old and bony
Allegro con variazione.'

A wee bird on an ivy spray
Said, 'Elaine's twenty-one today'
And little scherzos filled the air
Molto espressivo there
To see her growing day by day
Grazioso e dolcissime.

Alasdair Maclean

BRAMBLE PICKING

I went bramble picking all that autumn day,
finding out and stripping the hot hollows to the south,
the lazy basins that had known nothing but the sun, it seemed,
and the consideration of it, not its opposite and rival,
that white fruit-blanching colour-sucking radiance.

Brambles there were the first brambles ever picked.
Original to the place and native to the thick blue air,
they had an eden sheen to them. They were sunken brambles,
moored in the slow tides of endless flat-calm afternoons,
pulled down by their own weight till they touched bottom.

Everywhere were sheep, outwitted by the taste of bramble leaves,
Lured far into that dark and purple heat and caught,
they hung upon the stems like huge expensive blossoms.
Purple-fingered I milked the stems. I was unaffected.
I was myself cyclical and for the nonce at least content.

How well and swiftly I collected! It was all stoop and move
for a while, all touch and go; then the check came
of the pail's weight creeping slowly up my arm,
a chain of brambles shortening and snubbing as the tide rose;
then the notion growing from that of a centre or a source.

It was when I broached the deepest closest one,
a polyp of a hollow, fringed about the mouth with scrub
and foetid in its soft inside with rotting flesh,
a gulfstream forcing-house where every bush secreted brambles
and into which I lowered myself with leaden pail,

that I was stopped dead by the swarming horror of it all,
whelmed by a sudden need for cleanliness and love.
I dropped pail and brambles and surged upwards gasping.
When I broke the surface I was shouting out for help
as loud as I could carry. Over and over again I shouted.

SPRING SONG

The thaw came overnight and spring.
The mercury that had been curled
up in the bulb of the thermometer all winter rose
and all the yellow flags unfurled
and streamed the great deer herds
and from the locked branches freed the birds.
That man beyond my front window
who dreamed that he was king,
put off his robe of snow
and yawned and is again my old scarecrow,
the father of the field within a world
where all things flow.
Now, later by a month, I'd swear
that grass surmounted
everything that had been bare,
even in Kilchoan Churchyard
and even the amazing new grave there.

LITTLE BOY BLUES

I think that being the God of transcience
You pitied me, Lord, the lovely frail things
that took all my trust
yet did to them and me
what it was written down You must.
Now we are all changed and all free.
Sidi bel Abbes and the Legion smother
in a cloud of dust
and later harder dreams I had
that I was burgess of that golden land
where skin to skin the archetypal sweater clings,
they, too, were built on sand;
Miss Lana Turner's drooping bust
fills me in middle age with love, not lust.
Ah, well. You alter, too. But just
as You are I take You at Your word.
Now, when the flask of wine in my hand
trembles in the mornings
and I sit beneath a shadier bough,
catch me if You can, Lord.
Lord, You suit me now.

Trevor McMahon

HAD SHE DROWNED

Had she drowned I would have
scooped water from the pool
and washed my face and hands.

Had she suffocated I would have
taken feathers from the pillow
for my hair or worn them round

my throat as beads or charms.
But she had not suffocated or
been drowned, she breathed still.

regular and low, so that if I had
put a feather to her lips it would
have shivered in my hand as she

not long ago had shivered in my arms.
So as there was no drowning and she
breathed still, regular and low.

why were the legs spread,
and the arms awkward over the head,
and why the damp patch on the pillow?

Wes Magee

ROAD RUNNER

Simply, he ran to escape,
to cut loose from the strings and cabbage redolence
    of his home, the bitterness
of his father's failure. He lapped around the

    houses of his fist tight town,
zap zapped past head bent couples struggling against
    the rain, but always he circled,
gravitated home, and kicked off his sodden

    running shoes in the listing shed
that stood like a shroud over the skeleton
    of his brother's ancient car.
His anger sweated out, his disappointments

    doused, he entered again that
ill lit kitchen—another box on another
    estate. And for the years he
ran out the storm in his blood they pointed to

    his cowed look, the down swept mouth,
the silences, 'Miserable sod' they muttered
    and saw his loneliness stand out
like stigmata. Around the town's cage he ran

    to shake off the family snare,
driving the seasons into the iron ground,
    head down, legs pumping, fists clenched
white against the grey, the grey down beating rain.

Derek Mahon

A DISUSED SHED IN COUNTY WEXFORD

'Let them not forget us, the weak souls among the asphodels.'
Seferis, Mythistorema

for J. G. Farrell

Even now there are places where a thought might grow—
Peruvian mines, worked out and abandoned
To a slow clock of condensation,
An echo trapped for ever, and a flutter of
Wild flowers in the lift-shaft,
Indian compounds where the wind dances
And a door bangs with diminished confidence,
Lime crevices behind rippling rain-barrels,
Dog-corners for shit-burials;
And in a disused shed in County Wexford

Deep in the grounds of a burnt-out hotel,
Among the bath-tubs and the wash-basins
A thousand mushrooms crowd to a keyhole.
This is the one star in their firmament
Or frames a star within a star.
What should they do there but desire?
So many days beyond the rhododendrons
With the world waltzing in its bowl of cloud,
They have learnt patience and silence
Listening to the rooks querulous in the high wood.

They have been waiting for us in a foetor of
Vegetable sweat since civil-war days,
Since the gravel-crunching, interminable departure
Of the expropriated mycologist.
He never came back, and light since then
Is a keyhole rusting gently after rain.
Spiders have spun, flies dusted to mildew
And once a day, perhaps, they have heard something—
A trickle of masonry, a shout from the blue
Or a lorry changing gear at the end of the lane.

There have been deaths, the pale flesh flaking
Into the earth that nourished it;
And nightmares, born of these and the grim
Dominion of stale air and rank moisture.
Those nearest the door grow strong—
Elbow room! Elbow room!
The rest, dim in a twilight of crumbling
Utensils and broken pitchers, groaning
For their deliverance, have been so long
Expectant that there is left only the posture.

A half-century, without visitors, in the dark—
Poor preparation for the cracking lock
And creak of hinges. Magi, moon-men,
Powdery prisoners of the old regime,
Web-throated, stalked like triffids, racked by drouth
And insomnia, only the ghost of a scream
At the flash-bulb firing squad we wake them with
Shows there is life yet in their feverish forms.
Grown beyond nature now, soft food for worms,
They lift frail heads in gravity and good faith.

They are begging us, you see, in their wordless way,
To do something, to speak on their behalf
Or at least not to close the door again.
Lost people of Treblinka and Pompeii!
Save us, save us, they seem to say;
Let the god not abandon us
Who have come so far in darkness and in pain.
We too had our lives to live.
You with your light meter and relaxed itinerary,
Let not our naive labours have been in vain.

THE SNOW PARTY

Bashō, coming
To the city of Nagoya,
Is asked to a snow party.

There is a tinkling of china
And *saké* into china.
There are introductions.

Then everyone
Crowds to the window
To watch the falling snow.

Snow is falling on Nagoya
And farther south
On the tiles of Kyōto.

Eastward, beyond Irago,
It is falling
Like leaves on the cold sea.

Elsewhere, they are burning
Witches and heretics
In the boiling squares,

Thousands have died since dawn
In the service
Of barbarous kings;

But there is silence
In the houses of Nagoya
And the hills of Ise.

Paul Matthews

PIANO

Does the grandpiano still hum in the hallway
the way it did? 'Gathering honey', you said.

The strings vibrated each time a lorry passed
and at sherry-parties were resonant
for the very latest views about sponge-cake.

Would still be murmuring when the glasses were
all washed up and we'd gone to bed.

The mahogany lid was great for pulling faces in.

I only played black notes. 'Red-Indian music.'
Imagining dust-storms raised by their horses.

PHOTOGRAPH

In this photograph most of my relations
are sipping china-tea under the peartree.

That Summer was hot. The dragon teapot
steams on the table. I haven't seen it
since my grandfather died.
                              Be careful
not to break those fragile smiles. CLICK.

And the group scattered. To wash plates.
Others to die (but that was later).

One lady's head has escaped the picture
hoping to breathe.

John Mole

BATTLEGROUNDS

1

The scene: a military institution.
Soldier, lady guide, a squad of kids in scouting uniform,

a treat of sorts. 'This is the Bomb Room'
as one might say 'Our President slept here'.

The lady, shrill in tones of Sunday School—
'We call this little fellah Big Boy. Who

can tell me why we call him Big Boy?'
All hands up at once but one—

Again 'And who can tell me why we call him Big Boy?'
It is important to get straight about bombs.

A small voice stumbles amongst peers
'Because, because . . .' CORRECTION.

'What the kid means . . .' The soldier hesitates
then slaps the tonnage like a stallion's flank.

2

Lines for a B52
Tonight, I watch your load unfurl—
the ghostly patterns of a piano-roll.

What bright saloon, what double doors
Could hold the stranger in his tempered fury?

There where the music played, no fingers:
there while they shot it out the tempo could not change

and now the hidden children dance to ragtime,
babies cake-walk as you ride for home.

3

The scene: bereavement in another country.
One small coffin clutched to a father's chest like the groceries.

Stunned faces above dark suits: a violent grief
processing royally. The soldiers are discreet—

discreet, too, the cameras minding their business,
the shops closed. Mainly, it is the men one notices

and not O'Casey's stricken women, the flickering votive—
Something has passed beyond that, crossing borders

into the present. This is a different place
with the same tactics—the shattered pram, the journey home
                                        from school

and the child's voice answering 'Because, because . . .'
to questions raised by his own dying.

Slowly, without tears, he goes to a toy grave.
Meanwhile, the strategic placement of cordite.

John Montague

SMALL SECRETS

Where I work
out of doors
children come
to present me
with an acorn
a pine cone—
small secrets—

and a fat
grass snail
who uncoils
to carry his
whorled house
over the top
of my table.

With a pencil
I nudge him
back into
himself, but
fluid horns
unfurl, damp
tentacles, to

probe, test
space before
he drags his
habitation
forward again
on his single
muscular foot

rippling along
its liquid self-
creating path.
With absorbed,
animal faces
the children
watch us both

but he will
have none of
me, the static
angular world
of books, papers—
which is neither
green nor moist—

only to climb
around, over
as with rest-
less glistening
energy, he races
at full tilt
over the ledge

onto the grass.
All I am left
with is, between
pinecone & acorn
the silver smear
of his progress
which will soon

wear off, like
the silvery galaxies,
mother of pearl
motorways, woven
across the grass
each morning by
the tireless snails

of the world,
minute as grains
of rice, gross
as conch or
triton, bequeath-
ing their shells
to the earth.

Edwin Morgan

SCHOOL'S OUT

I

A colonnade, binding light in fasces
of striped stone and shadow, suited Plato.
'Tight reins,' he used to say, 'all training
is restraint.' Are boys like horses then?
Stupid questions got no answer, but
a thin smile came and went, left no trace.
We were born into Utopia:
cold baths, porridge and Pythagoras,
Pythagoras, porridge and cold baths.
We never exactly hated the routine
but felt there must be something else. He said
life should be in the Dorian mode, sober
as a shepherd's pipe, and 'hell take all
Bacchantes and Assyrian kettledrums',
which was strong words for him. Looking back,
it seems as if the discuses we threw
to swing our muscles into harmonies
'like the deep universe's harmonies'
were no more solid than the wrestling-oil
that seeped into the sand, or watery songs
of how the gods are good as gold. We did
our sums, deaf to the music of the spheres,
and came out into chaos,
blood, shrieks, kettledrums.

Milton thought a country house was best,
'at once both school and university',
and he'd have acres to do marvels in.
He was really pure theatre. I don't forget
his first words: 'Open your mouths, let me hear
a clear vowel from now on, stop mumbling
just because there's mist in Buckinghamshire.'
We thought he must be mad, but practical,
and it's no secret his model was Prince Hamlet
(bating the royal appurtenances).
We sweated swordplay, strategy and tactics,
as well as sonnets and the vocative.
We groaned through Hebrew but we knew the stars.
I could put on a splint, survey a field,
ride a horse and play the organ. Poachers,
pedlars, smiths he made us learn from, for
'you never know what might help the commonwealth'.
It's all gone now of course. The king came back.
Rigour was no longer *de rigueur*.
I sometimes wonder what it was all for—
and then I remember that sardonic voice
pausing in its anatomy lesson to say
    why heads of kings come
      off so easily.

3

Whatever did we learn at Summerhill?
No maths, no hangups; how to play *Dear Brutus*.
It wasn't doing barbola on the mantelpiece
with red-hot pokers, breaking windows all day
or maidenheads all night—though you'd think so
to hear the critics. And did Neill set us free?
You never know with voluntary lessons,
they crouch there in your path like friendly enemies,
you pat them or you sidle past, knowing
you can't play truant when you're free already.
School government was on our hunkers, noisy,
fizzing, seesawing, Neill won, we won, no one won
while the long shadows gathered on the chintz.
We were Hitler's autobahns in reverse,
anti-Stakhanovites, our trains would never
run on time. 'If I create a millionaire'
cried Neill 'I've failed!' But capitalism
slid on its way despite our lost repressions.
We tinkered in the workshop, made toy guns
but never robbed a bank or even knew
half Europe had been robbed. Now if you ask
what I think of it I honestly don't know,
    it was great but I
    honestly don't know.

Ivan Illich bought a big new broom.
'Most people learn most things out of school.'
Why not junk the institution then?
The point was we had reached the stage we could.
Access! access! was his cry, and timetables, textbooks,
exams, walls, bells were as much garbage
as last year's Cadillac. Plug in! playback!
tapespond! The electronic network longs
to set you free. The what and where and when
of learning's in your own hands now. Deschool.
Decamp. Disperse. The player and the game
are one, nobody prods men to the board.
—So we were the first tape and data children,
we've been through the tube, come out, still cool.
We know how Armstrong landed, bleeps call us
in our breast-pockets everywhere we go,
we've got cassettes of Basque folk-songs, slides
of the water-flea, microfilm drips from us
in clusters, if there's music of the spheres
we've heard it. I've been talking to the dolphins
in California, and they say they've seen
a school (which I know is impossible)
  far out in the bay.
  Whales, whales, you fool.

Robin Munro

PONIES

But you have to come back to Shetland
for the true strain.
They grow weak at the knees in France and in
Sussex meadows.
They degenerate.

They need the wind all the time,
the lift of the Scattald, the bare
mouthful of moor
cropped from the stone
tasting of flowers

and a salt whipping, force five 'Viking',
to fairly set them moving.

Like fire, they are not to be stopped.
But unlike fire, they are soon contented
in a different geometry
an unspoilt taste
and a same old world.

Leslie Norris

STONE AND FERN

It is not that the sea lanes
Are too long, nor that I am not
Tempted by the birds' sightless

Roads, but that I have listened
Always to the voice of the stone,
Saying: Sit still, listen, say

Who you are. And I have answered
Always with the rooted fern,
Saying: We are the dying seed.

BARN OWL

Ernie Morgan found him, a small
Fur mitten inexplicably upright,
And hissing like a treble kettle
Beneath the tree he'd fallen from.
His bright eye frightened Ernie,
Who popped a rusty bucket over him
And ran for us. We kept him
In a backyard shed, perched
On the rung of a broken deck-chair,
Its canvas faded to his down's biscuit.
Men from the pits, their own childhood
Spent waste in the crippling earth,
Held him gently, brought him mice
From the wealth of our riddled tenements,
Saw that we understood his tenderness,
His tiny body under its puffed quilt,
Then left us alone. We called him Snowy.

He was never clumsy. He flew
From the first like a skilled moth,
Sifting the air with feathers,
Floating it softly to the place he wanted.
At dusk he'd stir, preen, stand
At the window-ledge, fly. It was
A catching of the heart to see him go.
Six months we kept him, saw him
Grow beautiful in a way each thought
His own knowledge. One afternoon,
Home with pretended illness, I watched him
Leave. It was daylight. He lifted slowly
Over the Hughes's roof, his cream face calm,
And never came back. I saw this;
And tell it for the first time,
Having wanted to keep his mystery.

And would not say it now, but that
This morning, walking in Slindon woods
Before the sun, I found a barn owl
Dead in the rusty bracken.
He was not clumsy in his death,
His wings folded decently to him;
His plumes, unruffled orange,
Bore flawlessly their delicate patterning.
With my stick I turned him, not
Wishing to touch his feathery stiffness.
There was neither blood nor wound on him,
But for the savaged foot a scavenger

Had ripped. I saw the sinews.
I could have skewered them out
Like a common fowl's. Moving away
I was oppressed by him, thinking
Confusedly that down the generations
Of air this death was Snowy's
Emblematic messenger, that I should know
The meaning of it, the dead barn owl.

RAVENNA BRIDGE

Thinking he walked on air, he
Thrust each step, stretched straight
His ankle. We saw him lift
On thinnest stone between him-
self and earth, and then dip on.

Such undulant progress! Stern
Herons walk like that; but he
Just rose again into his
Highest possible smiling air,
Stepped seriously by us,

And kept for all himself
The edges, even, of his happiness.
Passing, we caught the recognition
Of his transfiguring sweet
Smoke, And so he stepped, he

Skipped, the thin boy, on narrow
Ravenna Bridge, itself a height
Over pines and sycamores. He
Danced above their heads. If
He hopped the handrail, had

Swayed into flight, fallen
To stony death among wood-doves,
We should have watched him. I did
Not stand as I felt, hand
To mouth in a still gasp, but

Coldly and relaxed, and saw the boy
Perform his happy legs across
Ravenna Bridge, and up the hill
To Fifty-Second. We walked home,
Thanking his god, and ours.

Robert Nye

READING ROBERT SOUTHEY
TO MY DAUGHTER

Mr Robert Southey had the makings of a haberdasher
With a candy-striped shop in Bristol or Bath,
A secondhand carriage and a bow-legged mistress
With Jacobin leanings; but ambition and his aunt
Drove him to verse
For which vice
He had no gift only
A self-consuming facility.

Mr Robert Southey had the honour
Of wearing the Coleridges as his albatross.
Bad Lord Byron made his name rhyme with mouthy
And dignified him with fire also
In his Vision of Judgment.

At worst Southey R was a creepy crawly
Using little epics as tickets of admission
To the lower reaches of what he thought society.
At best this esquire was a man who was better
Than any of his books. STC said
His library loved him.

O sweet O prolific O mediocre R
O ramblingly gallant and unimportant S
I remember how after the penultimate breakdown
Worn out with hacking you trotted up and down
Just stroking the spines
Of your seventeen thousand leather-bound concubines.

Mr Southey, man of letters, you worthy laureate
With such a thirst for righteous justice,
You once saw Shelley plain
And didn't care for it.
'What a dreadful thought of his wife's fate,'
You said, Sir, 'what a dreadful thought
Must have come upon him when he saw himself
About to perish by water!'
Mahomet was no better.

O Robert O Southey, if poor Percy Shelley
Screamed like a peacock, you clucked like a hen.
You had a fair heart but you geared it to royalties
And pensioned it off when the best time came.
Yet tonight, Robert Southey, I thank you by name
For the measure of a story you took and made better:
Not too fast, not too slow, not too hot, not too cold,
Not too hard, not too soft, not too long, not too short,
But just right for my Goldilocks—
Too young to say thank you
Herself, but who loves you
For loving just-rightness;
Bob of the Bears,
Our Southey friend.

HENRY JAMES

Henry James, top hat in hand, important, boring,
Walks beautifully down the long corridor
Of the drowned house just off Dungeness
At the turn of the century. It is 3 pm probably.
It is without doubt October. The sun decants
Burgundy through high windows. The family portraits
Are thirteen versions of the one face, walking
On the thick trembling stalk of Henry James.
It is a face which looks like the face of a goldfish
Fed full of breadcrumbs and philosophy, superbly
Reconciled to its bowl. The difference
Between Henry James and a goldfish, however,
Is that Henry James has nostrils. Those nostrils observe
An exquisite scent of evil from the library.
Henry James goes beautifully on his way. His step
Is complicated. (He nurses an obscure hurt. It is this
Which kept him from active service in the sex war.)
Listen and you will hear the trickle of his digestive juices—
Our author has lunched, as usual, well—
Above the sweetly unpleasant hum of his imagination.
His shoes make no squeak and he deposits no shadow
To simplify the carpet. Henry James
Turns a corner. Henry
James meets Henry
James. Top hat, etcetera. Henry James
Stops. Henry James stares. Henry James
Lifts a moral finger. 'You again!'
He sighs. 'How can you be so obvious?'
Henry James blushes and Henry James flees and Henry
James goes beautifully on his way, top hat
In hand, important, boring, he walks down
The long etcetera.

Valerie Owen

NICE PEOPLE

'Satire is less free than other forms of poetry because of its
necessarily close and immediate relation to the world of habit and
experience.'

*From H. V. D. Dyson's Introduction
to Pope's Poetry and Prose.*

When we got on to the platform
of the single shuttle line at Tilley-on-the-Hill,
Mother said the air was balm and she left her nervous
    breakdown
in the stationmaster's pigeon-hole.
After the first-night's supper they put away the thick china
and it was Limoges and chicken and the farm silver for us.
The other P.G. was Mr Tiney:
he put out his arms and breathed, 'Oh, you beautiful doll'.
Mother said, 'My little girl's fallen in love'.

Most of that summer I spent on Mr Tiney's knee
while round us the Erasmic soap
frothed madly in the soft water
and robins hopped in through the open door.
I awoke by the postage-stamp window
hearing cows low in the green Arras mud.
I leaped down the staircase in the cupboard,
hit my head on the last black iron-old beam
and fell stunned into Mr Tiney's waiting arms.

The next two summers we spent at the sea,
we had our own beach-hut, it was all Betjeman
and the smell of the spirit-stove, the hot meths
and doughnuts dropped in the sand. Then mother
felt nostalgia for Tilley-on-the-Hill,
for the windmill and the counties below
laid out like a mint-new sheet of stamps.
So we returned. Mr Tiney was again there
but he had brought his son, and another family
of P.G.s had come with two girls older than me
and one little one. Mr Tiney didn't take her
on his knee but he spoke to her all the time.
He didn't seem to have a wife but told mother
he was disappointed in his son who was seventeen.
Mother was disappointed in me too, for I had failed
to win a Free Place. It would have been Honorary
in my case she said, but I had let her down.

So I spent a lot of time in the orchard
where the rough-barked trees had an eau-de-nil deposit
while Mr Tiney stayed inside with the little girl
and the summer burned away.
I heard mother say, 'Mr Tiney doesn't like big girls',
and I looked down at my new breasts which like springs
trembled against the flat Elizabethan cotton chests
of the dresses which Mrs Newman still made for me,
while I rotted in the swing.

My mother doesn't go out any more. She is too old.
She says you must move with the times
but the P.G.s were nice people, now it's all
perversions and drugs. I try to remember Mr Tiney's face
in nine light shimmers which giggle on the wall.
I lift my eyes from psychology
and Charles Lutwidge Dodgson to watch a robin play.
The copper shows naked through mother's Sheffield Plate.
The wallflowers smell like Tilley Farm today.

Philip Pacey

CLEARING YOUNG BIRCHES

First, clear the ground of brambles,
brushwood, dead stems of heather. Lift
the mattock high and let it fall

in an arc from wrists'
centre; help it on its way
though its own weight's the main

force smashing into peat,
dragged from its dry crumbling. Hook
one fluke under an exposed root,

with the other a firm fulcrum haul
back from clenched feet till the sapling
shudders, gives, and you're careful

not to fall backwards in a wood ants' nest.
Repeat once, twice, at different points
till the tree's loose as a tooth that won't

out; grasp two armfuls of shoots, pull—
and marvel at the roots' horizontal
spread where the surface erupts, heather,

ferns, and wood sage are dislodged
that we press back into leafmould's
springiness. Or, more lazily,

all ache and losing patience, hack
through the slender trunk where it dives
deep; see how birch bleeds, where the bark chips

flake scarlet. Afterwards, how much delight
in walking from this work on the lookout
for woodpeckers! In the hall's calm sprawled

back to the wall where we sat to take boots off
minutes ago—held
still, not to spill well-being, so brimful!

William Plomer

CUPBOARD LOVE

In the front garden snowdrifts of snowdrops,
Predictable daffodils, floribund litterbug roses;
In the back garden leathery greens, then treasure-trove
New potatoes, wigwams of huge runner-beans.

Behind the front door Victor, no drop-out,
Rather a drop-in or opt-out, a marginal man,
An old man, with Beulah, the much older wife
Strangers supposed him, till put right, the son of.

It began back in 1914. Newly widowed,
Beulah married and mothered him. Victor,
A taciturn peasant, with nothing to lose but his life,
Demurred at the war. 'Take no notice,' she said.

'All will be over by Christmas. Till then
You can hide in that roomy great cupboard upstairs.'
Enwombed for four years; when he came out he remained
A homebody; went daily to garden at Atheling Grange,

Kept himself to himself, never seen in a pub or a club.
Someone did say: 'Victor, what happened to you in the war?'
'Never got through me medical, so was exempt.'
For fifty years more was exempt from the world.

When he followed its monstrous reflection in print,
On radio, then, caught in the act, televised,
He found it too wild to be false. 'I'm content
To be out of it all', he said, and very soon was.

Beulah survived him; somehow she knew that she would.
The earth is his hidey-hole now. The snowdrifts
Of snowdrops increase, and somebody else
Puts up the annual wigwams, and gathers the belt-like beans.

Peter Porter

SEASIDE PICNIC

Here where sprawl the armed persuaders,
   Denizens of three inch oceans
   Who rage as Genghis Khan over sand and rock
   Ignoring only the anemone's motions,
   Its meatless, beautiful tick-tock,
Here, scaled down from the world of waders,

Whose holiday gingerliness is as remote
   As God, the relentless law
   Renews itself: the soft-backed crab
   Ventures too far from its lodge, and claw
   and life both break at one stab
Of an old need and like seaweed are left to float.

This terror is enacted in seventy pools
   Of a single rock till the tide
   Renews like Deucalion's advance
   Another flood of darkness, and to hide
   Is the victim's and predator's equal chance—
This is a world without self-doubters or fools,

Egregiously unlike the pretty playground
   Of its kindhearted great
   Who might say to a clambering child
   'Don't leave that sea-snail to its fate,
   But right it on its shelf so the mild
Worm can cling, the life platform be sound.'

For they are swayed by such overreaching waters
   As they do not recognize
   Along the bristling beach on afternoons
   Of sun, and having learned to prize
   Hope, pass each other plates and spoons,
Unpacking love for their murderous sons and daughters.

Tully Potter

BLIND WOMAN

the blind woman who walked into me
stutters on up the hill,
pock-pocking with her long white wand

i wonder why we both said sorry,
though it seemed right

up she goes in her morse way,
stop-stopping at each gaggle
of squawking after-school children

leaving me
to find the right easy remark
—the right apology hardly off my lips,
the imprint of her squat body still on me
. . . and in my mind
something white frantically pock-pocking

WHO'S YOUR DADDY?

I see a great battleship moored in the snow
I see the silvery pencils of guns that bristle
I remake this image, I try to,
It is a pine-cone of lunar metal
Doors hinge in its steel, flakes fly,
Warm glows emerge
I see pollen
I see a pine cone consecrated to Attis
I see an ark
I know there are scrolls
Containing royal mysteries inside

Called explosives
Causing mysterious deaths understood by computer
It is a battleship
This will not be countermanded
It is a great battleship moored in the snow

It is not a white spider
Flying in its cracked web of the lake

It is not the discarded surplice
Of the summer-god, still warm inside

It is a battleship containing sailors
Trained to navigate and kill

It is no wedding-gown
Or wedding-blouse with golden buttons
From which light shines across snowy sheets
It is no iced honey-cake of the sacrament of marriage
In which the honey is sweet light
That will last a couple of years
Of married breakfasts

It is a battleship

Commanded

Metal commanded
By a man with steel-ringed eyes
By a man with golden wedded cuffs
Under orders

It is no felled yule-log
Stuffed with presents
The honey-log of a sedated bear

It awaits orders understood by computer
It does not guard us
It lives off us, dies because of us

It is the sledge made of dead men's nails,
The glittering horse of scythes,
The refrigerator of snowy carcasses.

SABBAT

come dancing
the men in black and white like governesses
the ladies clothed in sparking shrouds
unclothed at last!

so much money! no more need to work, or dress.

Mother has died and become the Food Hall at Harrods
with its French-cut veal, German Bratwurst,
langoustes and langoustines—

no washing up! no thousand sequins to polish
no shirts to boil
they live it up at last, foxtrot up and away

to their own music!

among the asses pastured in quiet among the hollies
the green-steel leaves and the hide-grey meadows
silver asses pastured in the moonlight

the synodic Bald Mountain lighted up
all the furrows and watercourses clean and brilliant

I hear the smoke bumping against the sides of the chimney
the freed witches bounding upwards, the palais empty.

Vernon Scannell

SPOT-CHECK AT FIFTY

I sit on a hard bench in the park;
The spendthrift sun throws down its gold.
The wind is strong but not too cold;
Daffodils shimmy, jerk and peck.

Two dogs like paper-bags are blown
Fast and tumbling across the green;
Far off laborious lorries groan.
I am not lonely, though alone.

I feel quite well. A spot-check on
The body-work and chassis finds
There's not much wrong. No one minds
At fifty going the speed one can.

No gouty twinge in toe; all limbs
Obedient to such mild demands
I make. A hunger-pang reminds
I can indulge most gastric whims.

Ears savour sounds. My eyes can still
Relish this sky and that girl's legs;
My hound of love sits up and begs
For titbits time has failed to stale.

Fifty scored and still I'm in.
I raise my cap to dumb applause,
But as I wave I see, appalled,
The new fast bowler's wicked grin.

SELF-INFLICTED WOUNDS

Soldiers who decided that
dishonour was a wiser
choice than death, or worse, and spat
into the face of Kaiser
Bill and the Fatherland or
King George's Union Jack
and took up their rifles for
the purpose of getting back
to Blighty by sniping at
their own big toes or trigger-
fingers were called things like 'rat'
but preferred scorn to rigor-
mortis and considered gaol,
for however long, a soft
touch after trench and shell-hole;
but it is only the daft
who think that self-inflicted
injuries hurt less than those
sustained by folk addicted
to being punched on the nose
or greeting mutilation
welcomingly for the sake
of glory and the nation.
The wounds and scars that ache
the worst, and go on aching,
are from blows delivered by
oneself; there's no mistaking
that sly pain, and, if you cry,
you cannot expect a breath
of sympathy; you will find
no healing of any kind
till he comes who began it
all, and cures all, Doctor Death.

Michael Schmidt

A HERMIT'S DREAM

I think it was I who found this thing—
stone-white among shell and shingle,
small as a thimble. If I picked it up,
I would have turned it in my palm, discovering
the holes that dripped cold water.
I would have held a tiny skull.

Like a bird's egg, oval,
thin as egg-shell, how the sea
which is not delicate had left it whole
perplexes me—it may not have come far
but it is clean as though it came from history,
and fine, as if an oriental craftsman

shaped it from white jade
and gave it to the sea.
It lets through light and has two sharp
parabolas of teeth—a carnivore's.
The jaw still works. There is
no trace of flesh, the eyes

were rainbows briefly, then spilled.
Empty, dry, and unlike conches, soundless,
it has no rightful place, no other bones.
It is like a hermit's dream
of being clean at last,
his body shared out to the elements,

become a vessel for some tide to fill.
I am no hermit and I do not dream,
but cupping it face-down in my palm
I think with my warmth
it could hatch out
a creature I would recognise, with wings,

a thing the sea and I would satisfy.
Turning it face upward I can choose
between a relic and a piece of time.
I watch a bone. I watch ancestors in its face.

Penelope Shuttle

CUPBOARD HYACINTHS

In the cupboard under the stairs
the winter flowers are crooning
in their cardboard pots

In the fierce dark
the roots of the hyacinth are stretching
their green havoc

I sit on the stairs
thinking of the garden beneath me
in the underworld of the cupboard

I think how handsome
my hyacinths will be,
how they will tower over December
with a fragrance as heavy as Isis

I will keep their corms from pestilence
because they contain my answers
Without the bending Pisas of their stems
I will have too many questions

I wait by the cupboard door,
I want to hear them grow,
I want to experience the cupboard's weather
I want to carry my lavender lamps
out into the winter rooms, to burn away scandals

Alan Sillitoe

FULL MOON'S TONGUE

She said, when the full moon's tongue hung out
Over the Earls Court chimney pots,
And he circled forever (slowly)
Round the square to find
A suitable parking place—

She said: Take me away: let's go together.

Keep clear, he said. You'd better not.
I'll take you, but watch out,
For I will bring you back, he said,
If at all,
In two pieces.

She said: I'll never want to come back
If I go away with you.

They all do, he said.
I'll bring you back in two pieces
And you'll live like that
Forever
And never join them up again.

How cruel, she said, seeing what he meant.

O no, he said, to take you apart completely
From yourself and make two separate pieces
Might be the one sure way of fixing
A whole person out of you—
If that's what you want.
Some do, some don't.
He was exceptionally nonchalant.

I'm not sure now, she said,
Screaming suddenly: You bastard.
Let me get out.
I want to walk.

He stopped the car
But could not park it,
Someone behind him with maybe a similar problem
Was hooting him to move,
So she jumped free and walked away
Leaving him bewildered
And in at least two pieces.

You talk too much,
Said one piece to another.

C. H. Sisson

A LETTER TO JOHN DONNE

Note : On 27 July 1617, Donne preached at the parish church of Sevenoaks, of which he was rector, and was entertained at Knole, then the country residence of Richard Sackville, third Earl of Dorset.

I understand you well enough, John Donne
First, that you were a man of ability
Eaten by lust and by the love of God
Then, that you crossed the Sevenoaks High Street
As rector of Saint Nicholas:
I am of that parish.

To be a man of ability is not much
You may see them on the Sevenoaks platform any day
Eager men with despatch cases
Whom ambition drives as they drive the machine;
Whom the certainty of meticulous operation
Pleasures as a morbid sex a heart of stone.

That you could have spent your time in the corruption of courts
As these in that of cities, gives you no place among us:
Ability is not even the game of a fool
But the click of a computer operating in a waste
Your cleverness is dismissed from this suit
Bring out your genitals and your theology.

What makes you familiar is this dual obsession;
Lust is not what the rutting stag knows
It is to take Eve's apple and to lose
The stag's paradisal look:
The love of God comes readily
To those who have most need.

You brought body and soul to this church
Walking there through the park alive with deer
But now what animal has climbed into your pulpit?
One whose pretension is that the fear
Of God has heated him into a spirit
An evaporated man no physical ill can hurt.

Well might you hesitate at the Latin gate
Seeing such apes denying the church of God:
I am grateful particularly that you were not a saint
But extravagant whether in bed or in your shroud.
You would understand that in the presence of folly
I am not sanctified but angry.

Come down and speak to the men of ability
On the Sevenoaks platform and tell them
That at your Saint Nicholas the faith
Is not exclusive in the fools it chooses
That the vain, the ambitious and the highly sexed
Are the natural prey of the incarnate Christ.

A GHOST

Nothing is more mysterious than a ghost. There are such
To be seen, between sleep and waking. Thomas Stearns Eliot,
For example, flashed between my eyelids and the waking room
And he was still there when I went downstairs,
Pottering among the books or admiring the view,
Quizzical, old, realising that there was little point
In his being there, but admitting that he had once met me
And so, a ghost had to do as he was told:
Tiresome, perhaps, but he put up with it.
He did not bother to go off down the garden
He would go, he knew, the moment my interest faded
And an old man could not be that interesting,
Above all to one already approaching those bournes
From which he had come. So he took his leave politely
As if raising his hat, at the very moment when I
Thought, after all, I would make myself some tea.

IN ARLES

The bitterness is covered but not buried
A little light earth, that is all
The centuries will not discover, nor the footfall
Be light upon me.

Lying there, in the light, unable to speak
No penny upon my lips
To send me thither to the Tartarus of time.
Have mercy, Lord.

My eyes open, the eyelids pulled apart
I stand here before time
Have mercy goddesses, standing in the long avenues
Death is in your keeping.

The bright eye, let me never be parted from it
I hear the drum now
I hear the whistle, there are pipes in this shrubbery
And the owl is near.

Pallas Athene, my dear
Look kindly upon my plain endeavours.
Light spins over the Camargue
Evening is here.

Christ of the mass-priests, farewell. Yet in the shadows
These have my tears
A crucifixion. a crucifixion, and the dogs howl
Nearer than death.

My tears, and my Saviour, this stone
The candle to light upon him
Eyes in the dark, the hidden light
And Pallas Athene is gone.

Yet she stands there at the entrance, smiling
The horses thunder by
—Is that money with which I cross her palm?—
I will come directly.

Iain Crichton Smith

SONNETS TO ORPHEUS

1

And he said, I am come in search of her
bringing my single bitter grief. I have
nothing more precious to offer
than this salt venom seeming to you as love.
It is true I cannot live without her
since I am now shade who was once fire.
See, mineral spirit, how I now suffer
by the slow heavy motion of my lyre.

And the god then replying: Let her stay
for by her absence your music is more clear,
barer and purer. Always in the air,
her distance will perfect her as idea.
Better the far sun of an April day
than fleshly thunder in the atmosphere.

2

And he said: That is great condemnation
to live profoundly and yet much alone.
To see deeply by a barren passion.
It was forgetfully I moved the stone
which now submits to my examination.
She was my sense: around her flowing gown
my poems gathered in their proper season.
They were her harvest yet they were my own.

And the god then replying: What you say
is what her absence taught you. Our return
is not permissible to an earlier way.
If it were possible you would learn to mourn
even more deeply. Do you never burn
poems whose language was becoming gray?

3

And he to the god: If you should let her go
I'd know my music had its former power
to melt you too as once it melted snow
to alter you as once it altered her
so that in music we both learned to grow.
It was a dance of earth and of the air.
But up above its easier. Here below—
The shade then smiled and said, 'Behold her there'.

And he beheld her whitely where she stood
in that deep shade. She seemed not to have changed
nor he to have changed either as he played.
And yet her apparition was so strange.
She didn't fit the music that he made,
the notes and she were mutually disarranged.

4

And the god to him: Now I must tell you clear
what you refuse to see (since it is hard
to accuse ourselves of cruelty and fear)
You wished that she should die. And what you heard
was not my voice but yours condemning her.
If you will learn to love you must go forward
For that is how it is in the upper air.
All that you have shared you have now shared.

And Orpheus took his lyre and left that place
and moved where the shadows moved, and the clouds flowed
and all that lived had its own changing grace
As on an April day there was sun and shade
but nothing vicious or virtuous
haunted the various music that he played.

EVERYTHING IS SILENT

Everything is silent now
before the storm.
The transparent walls tremble.
You can hear the very slightest hum
of a stream miles away.

The silence educates your ear.
The threat is palpable.
You can hear the boots behind the mountains.
You can hear the breathings of feathers.
You can hear the well of your heart.

You know what it is that permits the walls,
that allows the ceiling,
that lets the skin cling to your body,
that mounts the spiral
of your beholden bones.

That sorrow is a great sorrow
and leaves you radiant
when the tempest has passed
and your vases are still standing
and your bones are stalks in the water.

Stephanie Smolinsky

A CONSIDERED REPLY TO A MAN

Oh *man* are you saying that we're just like you?
You were born free. I was born in the zoo.

You'd have known it if you'd have grown up the same way,
the hands poked through bars, and the things people say.

And the eyes that keep watching whatever you do
you can't shit in peace, if you live in the zoo.

So that after a while, when they lock up at night,
It's as though they're still looking, you never feel right.

The eyes go on staring when you're all alone,
they shrivel your heart, and they turn it to stone.

But it's strange what the right clothes and make-up can do—
some folks never guess that I come from the zoo.

You can paint on a sneering, acceptable face
and strap my breasts in the appropriate place.

Disguise me with velvet and silver and lace . . .
a dozen Rag Markets might lend me some grace.

Invent me a style and a mind of my own
I'm almost a person, just look how I've grown.

And so independent, one hell of a show,
—but I don't contradict, and I never say no.

I've got techniques for everything you're going to see,
from licking your arse, to making your tea.

146

I'm good at insulting, I'm good at impressing,
at going to parties, at slowly undressing.

And I'm such a good listener, over the years
I've learnt to be quiet and now I'm all ears.

I draw you out beautifully, so sympathetic—
your agonised secrets . . . it's really pathetic.

We sit and you talk until quarter-past four,
and you'd never guess I'd heard it ten times before.

Oh, the tea and the friendship at four in the morning,
—while inside, my beast-self is scratching and yawning.

From my sensitive face to my sensitive cunt
YES FOLKS! you've got it! it's all one big front.

—But what am I saying? you know it's not true!
I'm just a dumb animal, born in the zoo.

I've tried to be human, I've bought me a soul,
I never make scenes, oh I've learnt self-control.

I'm the mirror you must have, the chorus, the clown:
your up's only measured by how much I'm down.

I'm the perfect companion, you won't find another—
you say you feel lonely? that's your problem, brother.

You've taught me your jargon; I speak it like you,
a bullet-proof glass screen, there's nothing gets through.

But you know my language, it sounds through your dreams,
the roars and the wolf-howls, the sighs and the screams.

You can stop writing letters, avoid conversations,
wear your coat and your boots during sexual relations.

You can black out your senses and block off your head,
beat up your own heart and leave it for dead,

lobotomise memory—O if you must
you can vomit your whole self up into the dust.

And still I exist. I'm the beast in your zoo
and my sharp eyes, my dumb eyes are fixed right on you.

No don't turn away, you, the animal-lover:
you come every Sunday, no need to take cover.

Here we are, face to face. Do you call me a cat?
A sow or a cow or a bitch or a rat?

Do you call me an equal? Do you make out I'm human?
Are you handing me babies and calling me Woman?

The zoo's everywhere—in this bed, in this room
the child we conceive touches bars in the womb.

I'm not after your pity, I don't need your need
there's a hole in my being no love's going to feed.

What's your good-will to me? would you go on all fours?
Man, could you un-man yourself in my cause?

It's too late for moods, for your ghastly caprice
I can't cringe any more, and I can't beg for peace.

It's too late for reason, it's too late for rage—
you can cut all the broadcasts, just open the cage.

And all that P. R.—shit about being my brother . . .
while my truth and your truth are killing each other.

We're crowding the cages, we're pressing the bars,
do you think your humanity's fixed in the stars?

Do you think we've begun our description of you?
What have we got to lose? We were born in the zoo.

Jon Stallworthy

IN THE ZOOLOGICAL SECTION

We stop in front of the case
containing skulls of two roe deer
who brought each other to this place.

Their antlers interlocked, they lie
eye-socket to eye-socket
as, starving, they lay eye to eye;

breath mingling as the hours pass,
eyes clouding over, like our own
reflected in the cabinet glass.

Anne Stevenson

PROFESSOR ARBEITER TO HIS DEAD WIFE

The worst time is waking
                        as if every nerve were working
scalpels in the running wound,   knives in the gash.
For in life, love, nothing begins or ends with a clean crash.
The brain knows, but habit is like cash or clothes.
It continues its momentum like a blind weight through glass.

I can't lie down in the dark with your severed voice, Ruth.
In this room full of trivial attentions I am still your guest.
'You're cold, dear. Let me fetch you your rug.'
'You're tired, I know. I'll tell them you need to rest.'
    Here.   Again.   On the phone.   Overheard in the hall,
'I'm sorry. My husband is working. At seven? I'll tell him
    you called.'

Ruth, in our thirty-six years lost to eye-strain and bad temper
you never spoke to me once of   what I know,
I neither dared nor dared not to speak to you,   though
sometimes your inattentions drove black words like swarming
    insects
swimming in held-back tears through my desperate paragraphs.

I was proud of you, Ruth.   My girl.
My critic.   My helpmate.   Hostess to a pack of fools
you could always smile at.   Confidante of students
too shy to seek me out.   Friend of all milkmen and maids.
One day.   One June, you gave tea to Isaiah Berlin.
                        And invited our Clearfield carpenter.

These last years have been . . . what, Ruth?

Living with someone who's dying.   Not letting her know.
And she, although not told,   knowing.
As though the courtesy of our mutual lie
was drawing us together under its canopy.

I read to you.   Henry Adams.   You had so much to say.
You asked for a handkerchief the last day.   Impatiently.
     As if death were a head cold.

I dream most nights of a garden.   Formal.   Like Versailles.
Laid out in terraces,   box hedges,   sculptured old
gods and goddesses.
                    We are walking together on a gravel path
when suddenly the vista changes.   Frames of ash
are descending in geometrical patterns
                                        to a dry fountain.

But the worst is waking.
Reaching for the radio through the strings of your voice.
Listening to the whining of hillbillies,   over and over,
               Closing my eyes
          as if the night could never be over.

A LONDON LETTER

The poet, Kay Boyd, Replies to her sister Eden in Vermont
Hampstead, November 11, 1968

          Your letter arrived with its letters
               lunging at my conscience.
               Alone in wet London

          with the wind trailing rain
               around these ugly brick villas
               and the four o'clock night

arriving with my late lunch,
  I ask myself often
    why it is impossible to go home?

Why is it impossible,
  even here,
    to be peaceful and ordinary?

The ordinary offers itself up,
  can be eaten, breathed in.
    It counts on being dependable.

This is a window.
  This is an apple.
    This is a girl.

And there is a cyclamen—
  blood climbing out of the ground.
    And there is a blind of rain.

And now between the girl
  and the flower-flame on the window sill
    the window is a blur of rainwater.

I wonder how she felt, Persephone,
  when she bit for ever into the half-moon pomegranate?
    Did she miss ordinary things?

She could have lived
  without risking the real fruit.
    There were only six seeds.

She willed to eat nothing else.
  It was hunger.
    Without nourishment how could she live?

Eating, she lived on through
    winter after winter,
        the long year perfected,

the cold, waking rain
    raising a few seeds to green
        from her creative darkness.

But the mother smiled and smiled.
    She was brilliantly consumed, a sacrifice
        sufficient for each summer.

Should any daughter blame her?
    The mother made her choice.
        She said her 'no' smiling.

She burned the kissed letters.
    She spat out the aching seeds.
        She chose to live in the light.

Would you wake her again from the ground
    where at last she sleeps
        plentifully?

R. S. Thomas

THE FLOWER

I asked for riches.
You gave me the earth, the sea,
                    the immensity
of the broad sky. I looked at them
and learned I must withdraw
        to possess them. I gave my eyes
        and my ears, and dwelt
in a soundless darkness
                  in the sunlight
        of your regard.
                  The soul
        grew in me, filling me
with its fragrance.
    Men came
to me from the four
        winds to hear me speak
        of the unseen flower by which
I sat, whose roots were not
in the earth, nor its petals the colour
of the wide sea; that was
        its own species with its own
        sky over it, shot
with the rainbow of your coming and going.

Anthony Thwaite

HEARING JAPANESE AGAIN

Liquid, glottal, with other sounds
Caught in the throat and gargled,
This speech avoids
The firm, peremptory plosives I know best.
The withdrawn hiss of concurrence or deference
Hovers over long-vowelled nods and becks,
The pause-words of politeness.

Raised to hieratic pitch, it comes through masks
Enunciating ghosts and demons,
Or with a plaintive monotonous whine
Is thought proper for children on the stage.
But this is conscious artifice—
The demotic is strange enough, heaven knows,
Heard in the street or floating into the garden.

Hearing it now again, after fifteen years,
The apartness of it chills and startles me
Like no other familiar but unlearnt tongue:
It is as if the air
Were full of the growl of feudal princeling doves
Making obeisance to a hawk that hovers
Above them, its beak impatient to stop the parleying.

Charles Tomlinson

THE WAY IN

The needle-point's swaying reminder
   Teeters at thirty, and the flexed foot
Keeps it there. Kerb-side signs
   For demolitions and new detours,
A propped pub, a corner lopped, all
   Bridle the pressures that guide the needle.

I thought I knew this place, this face
   A little worn, a little homely.
But the look that shadows softened
   And the light could grace, keeps flowing away from me
In daily change; its features, rendered down,
   Collapse expressionless, and the entire town

Sways in the fume of the pyre. Even the new
   And mannerless high risers tilt and wobble
Behind the deformations of acrid heat—
   A century's lath and rafters. Bulldozers
Gobble a street up, but already a future seethes
   As if it had waited in the crevices:

A race in transit, a nomad hierarchy:
   Cargoes of debris out of these ruins fill
Their buckled prams; their trucks and hand-carts wait
   To claim the dismantlings of a neighbourhood—
All that a grimy care from wastage gleans,
   From scrap-iron down to heaps of magazines.

Slowing, I see the faces of a pair
   Behind their load: he shoves and she
Trails after him, a sexagenarian Eve,
   Their punishment to number every hair
Of what remains. Their clothes come of their trade—
   They wear the cast-offs of a lost decade.

The place had failed them anyhow, and their pale
  Absorption staring past this time
And dusty space we occupy together,
  Gazes the new blocks down—not built for them;
But what they are looking at they do not see.
  No Eve, but mindless Mnemosyne,

She is our lady of the nameless metals, of things
  No hand has made, and no machine
Has cut to a nicety that takes the mark
  Of clean intention—at best, the guardian
Of all that our daily contact stales and fades,
  Rusty cages and lampless lampshades.

Perhaps those who have climbed into their towers
  Will eye it all differently, the city spread
In unforeseen configurations, and living with this,
  Will find that civility I can only miss—and yet
It will need more than talk and trees
  To coax a style from these disparities.

The needle-point's swaying reminder
  Teeters: I go with uncongealing traffic now
Out onto the cantilevered road, window on window
  Sucked backwards at the level of my wheels.
Is it patience or anger most renders the will keen?
  This is a daily discontent. This is the way in.

BADGER

Harmless they call him, a lovable nocturnal thing,
a family man spending daylight in his deep sett.
He has an old reputation for remaining aloof.
I thought he stuffed himself on insects and roots,
a fallen egg, a few mice, nothing his own size.
But from a cable-drum he came sniffing for our buck
after dark, baiting him and scratching at the mesh,
then deadly serious one night with his big jaws
and his bone-crushing molars rampant.
He wanted much more than a boring vegetable dish.

Grizzled snouter with the claws and thick white stripe,
he scooped a hole under the boxwood hutch,
splintered the floor with his ramming head
and then clambered up and through it.
Our poor young rabbit must have died of fright
but not before the badger minced him
into string and red slippery pulp.
That lovable thing left a smear of blood and droppings
on a mile-long strip of hutch and run
before a smallholder blew his head off.

W. Price Turner

READING POEMS OVER BRANDY

The illusion of fire and the fact of ice:
cold facets dwindle and the heat remains.
This is good brandy, and your poems are good
of their un-kind. I like the delicate clink
of the mind nudging its rigid limits. I admire
raw chunks of clarity cooped in refined
and pondered depths. Would a glass-blower,
spinning his glowing blob-fruit in the air,
care that the cooled glass matters less
than whatever it briefly contains? Yes
please, by all means replenish me. This
is excellent brandy, and I'll take a fresh
tundra, too. I think these images combine
splendidly. It's difficult to float
meanings without obscuring a fluid image,
and one can't mature potency overnight
like ice-cubes in a tray. Did I say
how much I enjoy the wry warmth of these
poems, the philosophical tone of this magnificent
brandy? You're sure you've plenty left?
I want to embark on a speculative blinder,
but I hope I know when I've had enough to read.
So let's end with a toast to the greatest need
of English literature, scruffy in its decline:
I mean more ex-poets, enough to start a trend,
and then more spirit to embrace the ice
that thins our blood. Press on, old friend,
your thumbs on the sweet eyeballs of the vine.

SITUATIONS VACANT (WOMEN)

From little girls with butterfly bows that crown
their first sweep of hair, to old ladies dragging
badly packed bundles of flesh, lagging
what's left of the slow spirit, I go down
between sparkle and haze. From eyes unseeing
back to eyes ripe for comprehension, range
that constant infinity of changes
where I construe the grammar of my being
in its profoundly useless declensions.
From the past partable, to the present
partial and future participant, I marshal
my pangs and sighs and partisan tensions
to praise the eternal ephemeral parades
of femininity, modesty, or wanton grace,
though not one is satisfied with her own face.
I swear that no matter how often betrayed
by the beauty of women it is only
wilful ugliness that's hard to condone.
Grudges sullying a near perfect bone
structure will ensure a bitch stays lonely.
But the sweet duplicities have taken their toll.
Though I still look backward at a booted stride
I no longer cater to prima donna pride
or supply therapy for the maladjusted soul.
Let frustrated wives lavish come-hither
looks on other men. The indelicate marks
of passion have faded, and those tiny sparks
of static longing rouse merely a token dither.
So the vacancy being advertised here
may be termed of a challenging nature.
Wanted, warm-hearted woman, as fellow-creature
to share music and silence. She'll be sincere,
responsive, good-humoured, free from worry.
Don't waste postage: apply personally. Hurry!

Jeffrey Wainwright

THE MIGRANT FROM ENGLAND

1

A rusty sign and tire tracks
E–Z OFF   E–Z ON

He has a limp now and a scar
and his teeth are plugged

What do you do where nothing grows,
sell cigarettes?

Nope. Beer and whiskey
if your money's good
just beer and whiskey

2

When my wife left
I had just my two sons—
my gospel children.

One of them walked out
when he was sixteen
—never a word—
and came back
six years later.
Hullo Dad he said
. . I threw him out.

The other still lives
to the north of here
and calls on holidays.
He has no sons and no wife.

3

when death shall close mine eyes

I saw a book in a store once
a picture of an old Indian in it
left by all his tribe in a cave
or some hole in the rock

I'm no Indian
shouldn't have to end up that way
in this shack, a filling station,
or any other damn place

4

I knew a man once who'd say

Praise the Lord who will help Man
Make Paradise of this Earth!

'It's possible, you know,' he used to say,
'It's possible.'

5

In deserts, they say the Sun is Hell
And the Moon is Paradise,
And that's the way I've found it.

That sign lights up at night for Rheingold
And it's more than a rush candle to me
Coming back from a piss in the dark.

I'm looking westward
'cause that's where the sun sets
Down and a-cries to hisself.

THE SILVER EAGLE

Map tables of veined marble; state rooms; desks; clerks.
The Secretary of State comes in at three.
It is November: his aide puts on the lights.
Rinses his cup and saucer and sets them out.

War is to be detested for its savagery.
If cannons boom once more in the Medway towns
Think of the domestic misery that will ensue.
But men are happy; the brute world soluble.

A silver eagle perched on Wilhelm's beaver
A silver eagle melted from an inkstand
Shrieks

'*No, that is not true!*
I warn you that is not true!'

Andrew Waterman

IT CAME ABOUT

It came about. He lay and smoked and watched
her kneel to brush her hair, against sky
stamped with high leaves' black perforations. Dressing,
she showed a pale tar-stain that occluded
the round of her knee, from a childhood fall.

So it happened he often came to lie
beneath sliding blankets in her attic room,
where sparrows brawled in the gutter. The season turned:
one night he leaned from the flesh-warm bed
through the window, to snap off icicles.

Years later, it came about that he met her again,
at a party. They talked of their children, schools;
it seemed she still had her career. He liked her.
Might they not become friends? That night
he dreamed of the small blue translucence clouding a knee.

Jane Wilson

I GO FOR NAPOLEONS

I go for Napoleons, for small
men with chips on their shoulders, which they take
the opportunity to carve beautifully,
like Alpinists in a bad winter;
who are working out their Thing in attics, who need helping
who command absolutely battalions in piazzas;
who wear size 6 in suede, so terribly hard to get;
who have Beethoven hair which I brush, brush after,
and look for singly when they are gone.

Small men, with understated chests and hidden vests
of their own forests; jockeys
who thunder aggression in suitable places, and
whittled men, whose eyes are pricked, and who think
before speaking, then don't speak, leaving
you guessing; who know the body under the dress
and the mind under the bone; men
who come to you for rest, rest
beyond communication;
who have ordered their lives and the wine
and the undertaker;

        and I ache
for the oppressed, the trodden, yes, and all of us in
this progressive rat-race to the cliff-edge;
and so salute our brothers, the far small
swamped ones, who must bend the forest
for shelter, who are servants of their neighbours
by choice, who live at peace, who are
small diners in a gross saloon—
the dark survivors.

STILL LIFE

This carboy has two
Thick ears I can stick
My nosey finger through.

The wine, like a homing bat
Goes what what what
Into its plastic top hat.

Roll on the solution
With health or mud in your eye!
This is an unfiltered generation.

Its dark hunch can send
One's own reflection out of all
Proportion round the bend.

But there's a highlight most
Times on the side
Tall as a holy ghost.

THE CONTRIBUTORS

FLEUR ADCOCK was born in Papakura, New Zealand, in 1934. he was educated at numerous schools in England and New Zealand and t Victoria University of Wellington, N.Z., where she read classics. Since 963 she has been settled in London and works as a librarian in the Foreign nd Commonwealth Office. Her publications include *Tigers* (1967), and *ligh Tide in the Garden* (1971), both published by Oxford University ress. A new collection, *The Scenic Route*, is due late in 1974.

JAMES AITCHISON received an Eric Gregory Award for poetry 1968, and his collection, *Sounds Before Sleep* (Chatto & Windus) won a lew Writing Award from the Scottish Arts Council in 1973. He was ducated at the Universities of Glasgow and Strathclyde, where he gained is doctorate for a thesis on Edwin Muir. James Aitchison has worked as a opywriter, a journalist and a teacher, and he is currently the Fellow in reative Writing in the University of Strathclyde.

W. H. AUDEN, who died last year, was born in 1907 and educated at iresham's School and Christ Church, Oxford, and in 1937 won King ieorge's Gold Medal for Poetry. He became a United States citizen in 946. His books include: *The Orators; The Dance of Death; The Ascent of '6, The Dog Beneath The Skin* and *On The Frontier* (with Christopher sherwood), *Look, Stranger; New Year Letter; For The Time Being; The ge of Anxiety; Nones; Homage to Clio; The Dyer's Hand; About the louse; A Certain World: A Commonplace Book; Epistle to a Godson and ther Poems*.

EDWARD BARKER was born in 1908 in Yorkshire's West Riding. Ie was trained in theology at Manchester. His vocation as a Methodist inister was cut short by carcinoma of the vocal cords. Deprived of his aritone voice, he trained in analytic psychotherapy and for the past uarter of a century has sustained a busy private practice in psycho-erapy in Hove, Sussex. He is a member of the British Association of sychotherapists, and his publications include *Psychology's Impact on the hristian Faith*, and '*Nerves*' *and their Cure* (Allen & Unwin).

EAVAN BOLAND was born in Dublin in 1944; took a first in nglish literature at Trinity College, Dublin, and taught there as a Junior ecturer for a while. Has published one book of poetry, *New Territory* ʲiggis; Dublin) and is finishing a second, *The War Horse*. In 1968 got a lacaulay Fellowship in poetry from the Irish Arts Council and now lives Dublin, married to the novelist Kevin Casey.

EDWIN BROCK was born in London in 1927, and now lives in Norfolk. Since his first collection in 1959, he has published five further collections in this country and America, the most recent being *The Portraits and the Poses* (Secker & Warburg, London; New Directions, New York). *Here. Now. Always.*, an autobiographical sequence of prose and poetry, is due from the same two publishers next year. He has been poetry editor of *Ambit* for more than ten years, and a selection of his poetry appears in *Penguin Modern Poets No. 8*.

GEORGE MACKAY BROWN was born in Stromness, Orkney, in 1921. He attended Newbattle Abbey College and Edinburgh University. He has published four volumes of verse, two novels, a play, and three books of stories (all from Hogarth); and a book on Orkney (Gollancz). He lives all the time in Orkney.

WAYNE BROWN was born in Trinidad in 1944. He read English at the University of the West Indies, Jamaica. His first collection of poems *On the Coast* (André Deutsch, 1972), was a Poetry Book Society recommendation.

TOM BUCHAN was born in Glasgow in 1931 and educated there and in Aberdeen. He has published three books of poetry and also works as a playwright and theatre director, best known as the co-author with Billy Connolly of *The Great Northern Welly Boot Show*. He was Professor of English at Madras University in the fifties and Warden of Community House, Glasgow, 1958–60. Until 1970 he was Head of the Department of English at Clydebank Technical College. At present he is editor of the Scottish monthly *Scottish International*.

CHARLES CAUSLEY was born in 1917 at Launceston, Cornwall. He served in the Royal Navy from 1940 to 1946. His books of verse are *Farewell, Aggie Weston* (1951), *Survivor's Leave* (1953), *Union Street* (1957), *Johnny Alleluia* (1961), *Underneath the Water* (1968), *Figure of 8* (1969) and *Figgie Hobbin* (1971). A selection of his poems appears in *Penguin Modern Poets 3*. He has also written *The Tail of the Trinosaur* (1973), a story in verse for children, He has edited a number of verse anthologies, the most recent being *The Puffin Book of Magic Verse* (1974). He was awarded the Queen's Gold Medal for Poetry in 1967, and received the Cholmondeley Award for Poetry in 1971. He has taught for over twenty-five years in his native town, and was appointed Honorary Visiting Fellow in Poetry at the University of Exeter for 1973–4.

GILLIAN CLARKE was born in Cardiff of Welsh-speaking parents and educated in South Wales. She read English at University College Cardiff then, for two years, worked for the B.B.C. in London. She returned to South Wales, was married and took up part-time lecturing. Since 1972 she has been Reviews Editor of the *Anglo-Welsh Review*. She began writing poetry in 1971 and her first collection, *Snow on the Mountain*, was published in 1972 (Christopher Davies). Since then her poems have appeared in a number of magazines, including *Poetry Wales*, *the Anglo-Welsh Review* and *Poetry Now*.

TONY CONNOR was born in 1930 in Lancashire. He left school at fourteen and worked for the next sixteen years in the textile industry. In 1962 he published his first book of poems, *With Love Somehow*. This was followed by *Lodgers*, 1965, and *Kon in Springtime*, 1968. From 1967 to 1969 he lived in the U.S.A. where he acted as writer in residence at Amherst College, Mass., and Wesleyan University, Conn.

JOHN COTTON was born in London in 1925. From 1962 to 1972 he was editor of *Priapus*. His collection, *Old Movies and Other Poems*, published by Chatto & Windus, was a Poetry Book Society recommendation and won an Arts Council publication award. He is currently editor of *The Private Library* and chairman of the Poetry Society. He lives with his wife and two sons in Berkhamsted.

KEVIN CROSSLEY-HOLLAND was born in 1941. His collection of poems, *The Rain-Giver*, was published by André Deutsch in 1972. He has translated *Beowulf* and many of the Old English shorter poems and written a book about eight British Islands, *Pieces of Land*, and a number of books for children. He once helped to cultivate the poetry list at the House of Macmillan (Sag mir wo die Blumen sind), and is now editorial director of Victor Gollancz Ltd.

DONALD DAVIE was born in 1922 and educated at Barnsley Holgate Grammar School and St. Catherine's College, Cambridge. He has been a Fellow of Trinity College, Dublin, and of Gonville and Caius College, Cambridge. Since 1968 he has been Professor of English at Stanford University, California. His more recent publications include *Ezra Pound: Poet as Sculptor*, and *Collected Poems, 1950–1970*. His recreations are verse translation, literary politics and travel.

173

PETER DENT was born in London in 1938 and educated at Egham and Berkshire College of Education. He did his national service in the R.A.F., is married, and is now learning and teaching in Surrey. His work has been published in *Agenda, Lines Review, Meridian, Sarphire*, the *New Statesman, Tribune* and other periodicals. A collection of his poems *Proxima Centauri*, was published in 1972, and a further volume, *The Time Between (Poems from the Chinese and others)* will appear in 1974.

ALAN DIXON was born in Liverpool in 1936. He is the author of two collections of poems, *Snails and Reliquaries* (Fortune Press, 1964) and *The Upright Position* (Poet & Printer, 1970). His work has been published in *New Statesman*, the *Listener, The Times Literary Supplement* and elsewhere. After National Service in the R.A.F. he attended Goldsmiths College. His other creative obsessions are painting and drawing, and he has taught art in secondary schools in London and Peterborough. He has a third book-length collection ready for publication somewhere.

DOUGLAS DUNN was born in 1942, and until 1964 lived in Inchinnan, Renfrewshire. He has published *Terry Street* (Faber, 1969), *The Happier Life* (Faber, 1972), *A Choice of Lord Byron's Verse* (Faber, 1974) *Love or Nothing* (Faber, 1974), and *British Poetry* (Antaeus, No. 12, 1973) He edited the last P.E.N. anthology, *New Poems 1972-73*. He is married and lives in Hull, working as a freelance writer.

D. J. ENRIGHT returned to England recently after twenty years of teaching in the East and now works in publishing. Publications include *Memoirs of a Mendicant Professor* (1969), *Selected Poems* (1969), *Shakespeare and the Students* (1970), *Foreign Devils*, poems (1972), *Daughters of Earth*, poems (1972), *Man is an Onion* (literary essays) (1972) and *The Terrible Shears*, poems (1973).

GAVIN EWART was born in London in 1916, and educted at Wellington College and Christ's College, Cambridge. He has worked for the British Council and as an advertising copywriter. His first poems were published in *New Verse* in 1933 and his books include *Poems and Songs* (1939), *Londoners* (1964), *Pleasures of the Flesh* (1966), *The Deceptive Grin of the Gravel Porters* (1968) and *The Gavin Ewart Show* (1971). Due this summer are *Be My Guest*, (Trigram Press) and *Penguin Modern Poets No. 25*, which includes his work.

ROY FISHER was born in Birmingham in 1930 and teaches in the Department of American Studies at Keele University. He is married, with two sons. His books are *The Ship's Orchestra* (1967), *Collected Poems* (1969), *Matrix* (1971) and *The Cut Pages* (1971). The most recent of his other publications is *Bluebeard's Castle* (1972), a collaboration with the artist Ronald King.

ROGER GARFITT was born in 1944, and was educated at Tiffin School, Kingston upon Thames, and at Oxford. Now teaching part-time at the Oxford College of Further Education, and writing freelance. Poetry critic of the *London Magazine*. Fiction Reviewer for *The Listener*. Pamphlet *Caught on Blue* in Carcanet Press series. First hardback collection due from Carcanet, October 1974. Critical essay in *British Poetry Since 1960* (Carcanet, 1972). Winner of the 1973 Guinness International Poetry Competition at the Stroud Festival, and of the Dorothy Mauger Award at the Portsmouth Festival.

RAYMOND GARLICK is an Anglo-Welsh poet and—apart from occasional publication in the Netherlands, where he lived for some years, and in the U.S.A.—rarely publishes outside Wales. His Collected Poems, *A Sense of Europe* (Gwasg Gomer, 1968), contained work from a number of previous books, and was followed by *A Sense of Time* (Gomer, 1972). Both volumes received a Welsh Arts Council poetry prize, and poems from them are recorded on one side of an Argo disc (PLP 1156). He has also written *An Introduction to Anglo-Welsh Literature* (University of Wales Press, 1972).

VALERIE GILLIES was born in Alberta, Canada, in 1948, and educated in Edinburgh, where she graduated with an Honours degree in English Literature. Awarded a Commonwealth Scholarship, she attended the University of Mysore, South India, as a postgraduate student of Indian writing in English. After a year living in India, she returned to Scotland to train as a teacher. She has contributed poems to the *Scotsman*, *New Edinburgh Review*, *Ariel*, and *Scottish International*. Married to a Celtic scholar, she has settled in Scotland and has a one-year-old son.

HENRY GRAHAM is a lecturer at Liverpool Polytechnic. Poetry Editor for the magazine *Ambit*. Published collections: *Soup City Zoo*, Anima Press, 1968, *Good Luck To You Kafka/You'll Need It Boss*, Rapp & Whiting, 1969, *Passport to Earth*, André Deutsch, 1971, Contributed to many international anthologies. *Anthologies in England*, *The Liverpool Scene*, *Love Love Love*, *British Poetry since 1945*, *Come on Everybody*, P.E.N.'s *New Poems 1971–72*, *The House that Jack Built*. Awards: £500 Arts Council award for the 1969 collection, and £550 Arts Council award for the 1971 collection.

THOM GUNN was born in Gravesend in 1929. His fifth book of poetry *Moly* was published in 1971. He has lived for some years in San Francisco.

MICHAEL HAMBURGER was born in Berlin in 1924. He emigrated to England in 1933 and was educated at Westminster School and Christ Church, Oxford. Between 1951 and 1964 he lectured in turn at the Universities of London and Reading, resigning a readership in German at Reading in 1964 in order to devote himself to full-time writing. In addition to numerous contributions to literary and scholarly journals, his publications include translations, several critical works and collections of his own poetry. His recent publications are *Ownerless Earth* (new and selected poems), *A Mug's Game*, *Intermittent Memoirs* and the bilingual anthology *East German Poetry*, all published by Carcanet Press; and *Hofmannsthal: Three Essays* (Princeton University Press).

SEAMUS HEANEY was born in 1939 in County Derry. He worked in Belfast until 1972 when he moved to County Wicklow. His published works include *Death of a Naturalist* (1966), *Door into the Dark* (1969), and *Wintering Out* (1972). In 1973 he received the American–Irish Foundation's Literary Award.

LOIS MARCH HERRICKSON lives in London and works in verse and prose, trying to develop in both disciplines a style and form which will help to bring literature out of its current impasse.

DAVID HOLBROOK has published four books of verse, *Imaginings*, *Object-relations*, *Against the Cruel Frost* and *Old World New World*, also a novel, *Flesh Wounds*. He is author of six books on the teaching of English, eleven on the psychology of culture, and is compiler of nine anthologies. He is married with four children and is Assistant Director of English Studies at Downing College, Cambridge. His best-known work is *English for the Rejected*; and he is well known as an opponent of pornography, especially because of its corruption of children. He is working on three new novels, a volume of eighty poems, three books on cultural nihilism, and further studies of psychology, on Gustav Mahler and Sylvia Plath.

GLYN HUGHES was born in Middlewich, Cheshire, in 1935. Studied painting at Regional College of Art, Manchester. Apart from several pamphlet collections, his main books of poems are *Neighbours* (1970), which was a Poetry Book Society recommendation and was awarded a prize by the Welsh Arts Council; and *Rest the Poor Struggler* (1972), both published by Macmillan. His most recent work is *Northerners* (a prose book on the millstone-grit area of the Pennines), to be published by Gollancz in 1975. At present he lives in Yorkshire, mainly by giving poetry readings.

TED HUGHES was born in Mytholmroyd, West Yorkshire, in 930, and from Mexborough Grammar School went to Pembroke College, Cambridge. His publications include *The Hawk in the Rain* (1957), *upercal* (1960), *Meet My Folks!* (1961), *The Earth-Owl and Other Moon eople* (1963), *How The Whale Became* (1963), *Nessie the Mannerless Monster* (1964), *Wodwo* (1967), *Poetry In the Making* (1968), *The Iron Man* and *Crow* (1970). He was married to the late Sylvia Plath, and now ves in Devonshire with his second wife Carol and his two children.

ELIZABETH JENNINGS was born in Lincolnshire in 1926 and ducated at Oxford High School and at St. Anne's College, Oxford. From 950 to 1958 she was Assistant Librarian in Oxford City Library, later orking for Chatto & Windus as an editorial assistant, but now devotes er time to her own writing. She has published five books of poetry, the rst winning an Arts Council Prize, the second the Somerset Maugham ward of 1956. With Dannie Abse and Stephen Spender she edited the th P.E.N. anthology, *New Poems, 1956*. Other books have included *he Mind Has Mountains* (poems, 1966), *Collected Poems, 1967*, *The nimals' Arrival* (poems, 1968). Also, poems for children, *The Secret rother* (1966). She won an Arts Council Bursary in 1969 and published *ucidities* (poems) in 1970. Latest works are *Relationships*, a book of poems 1972), and a critical, biographical study of Gerard Manley Hopkins hich is coming out in the U.S.A. very soon.

GEORGE KENDRICK, a thirty-nine-year-old lecturer at the ull College of Technology, is married, with two children. His poetry as been published in England and America, and broadcast by the B.B.C. . pamphlet, *Erosions*, has been published recently in the Phoenix Pamph- t Poets series. A book is now out.

GEORGE MACBETH was born in Scotland in 1932, and educated t New College, Oxford. He now works for the B.B.C. His books include *he Colour of Blood* (Macmillan, 1967), *The Night of Stones* (1968), *A Var Quartet* (1969), *The Penguin Book of Victorian Verse* (1968), *The urning Cone* (1970), *Collected Poems 1958–1970* and, most recently, *My cotland* (1973) and *A Poet's Year* (1973). He is married and lives in ichmond, Surrey.

NORMAN MACCAIG'S published works (all poems) are: *Far ry, The Inward Eye, Riding Lights, The Sinai Sort, A Common Grace, A ound of Applause, Measures, Rings on a Tree, Surroundings, A Man in My osition, Selected Poems* (Hogarth), *The White Bird* and *Penguin Modern oets, 21*. He has edited *Honour'd Shade* (anthology of Contemporary cottish Poetry) and co-edited with Alexander Scott, *Contemporary cottish Verse, 1959–69*.

ALASDAIR MACLEAN was born in Glasgow in 1926. He le
school at fourteen, and had various jobs in this country and elsewher
He graduated Edinburgh University four years ago with a degree i
English. Since then he has earned living as freelance writer and been
regular contributor of poetry to various outlets. His collection entitle
From the Wilderness was published last year by Gollancz (Poetry Boo
Society Choice).

TREVOR MCMAHON was born in Belfast and educated at tl
Royal Belfast Academical Institution and the Queen's University of Be
fast, where he is at present finishing a B.A. in English Language an
Literature. He began writing at school and has published erratically i
England and Ireland and on radio since then. With William Peskett l
founded *Caret*, a poetry magazine, in 1972, and with him continues t
edit it.

WES MAGEE was born in Greenock, Scotland in 1939. At prese
working as a Junior School teacher in Swindon; and as winner of Ne
Poets Award for 1972 his first volume *Urban Gorilla* was published t
Leeds University Press. Previously he was included in Faber & Faber
Poetry Introduction: 2. Also writes short stories, and is working on a nov
for children.

DEREK MAHON was born in Belfast, 1941, educated at Trini
College, Dublin, and now lives in London. Has published *Night-Crossi*
(1968), a Poetry Book Society Choice, and *Lives* (1972).

PAUL MATTHEWS was born in 1944. He is married with tw
children. He gained an English degree at Sussex University and whi
studying in Brighton he worked with George Dowden and edited *11
Finger* with Paul Evans. Later he trained in the Rudolf Steiner educatic
methods at Emerson College in Sussex, where at present he is teachi
experimental writing. He gives poetry readings, and his work has a
peared widely in magazines and anthologies, including *Children of Albi*
(Penguin), and *C'mon Everybody*, (Corgi). Several booklets of his poet
have been published.

JOHN MOLE was born in 1941 in Somerset, and educated at King
School, Bruton, and Magdalene College, Cambridge. His poems ha
appeared in various magazines and periodicals, including *New State
man*, *Encounter*, and *Phoenix*, and have been broadcast by the B.B.C. H
first collection, *The Love Horse* (E. J. Morten), was published in 1973, ar
a new volume, *Before the Storm*, has now been completed. He is c
editor of *Cellar Press Poems* (Hitchin, Herts) and a member of the Easte
Arts Association's *Writers in Schools* project.

JOHN MONTAGUE was born in 1929. Educated Armagh and University College, Dublin. Has published two collections of poetry, *Poisoned Land* (1961) and *A Chosen Light* (1967), as well as a collection of stories, *Death of a Chieftain* (1964) (all from MacGibbon & Kee), *Tides*, a collection of poems published by Dolmen Press (1971), a long poem on his native Ulster, *The Rough Field* (Dolmen/Oxford, 1972), and *A Fair House*, translations from the Irish (Cuala Press, 1973). He edited *The Faber Book of Irish Verse* in 1974. A freelance writer and academic (ranging from Berkeley to the Experimental University of Vincennes), he is now lecturing at University College, Cork.

ROBIN MUNRO was born on the Island of Bute in 1946. He was educated in Galloway and at Aberdeen University. He combined writing with a number of jobs and came to Shetland as a nature warden with the R.S.P.B. He has since lived between there and north-east Scotland. In 1973 he received a Scottish Arts Council Bursary and in the same year a limited edition of his poems, *Shetland, Like the World*, appeared.

LESLIE NORRIS was born at Merthyr Tydfil in 1921. Has published six books of verse, including *Mountains Polecats Pheasants*, which Chatto & Windus brought out recently. Winner of the Poetry Society's Alice Hunt Bartlett Prize for 1971 with *Ransoms*, an earlier collection. Was Visiting Poet at the University of Washington in 1973 and is Chairman of Southern Arts Association's Literature Panel.

ROBERT NYE was born in London in 1939 and educated at state schools, 1944–55. He contributes critical articles and reviews to periodicals, notably the *Scotsman*, *The Times*, and the *Guardian*. Since 1967 he has been Poetry Editor of the *Scotsman*; and since 1971 Poetry Critic of *The Times*. He lives in Edinburgh, is married to the painter Aileen Campbell, and has six children, His most recent collection of poems is *Darker Ends* (1969); he has also published a novel, *Doubtfire*, a book of short stories, *Tales I Told My Mother*, and prepared editions of Ralegh, Swinburne and William Barnes. The text of his masque, *The Seven Deadly Sins*, which goes on at this year's Edinburgh Festival (with masks by his wife and music by James Douglas) has just been published by the Omphalos Press.

VALERIE OWEN was born in Essex where her father taught Art and Crafts. She studied at the Slade School of Fine Art and the Institute of Education, University of London, and has taught Art and Liberal Studies in Secondary Schools and Colleges. She wrote poetry only very sporadically until the past three or four years during which she has won prizes for poetry collections and been both short-listed and a runner-up for the New Poets Award. She has also written a short radio verse play and a novel.

PHILIP PACEY was born in Yorkshire in 1946 and educated a
Hitchin, Bath, and at Corpus Christi College, Cambridge. Traine
in librarianship at the College of Librarianship, Wales, Aberystwyth
Tutor Librarian at St. Albans School of Art since 1970. Poems an
criticism published in a variety of magazines and anthologies, notabl
Poetry Review, *Poetry Wales*, *Second Aeon*, *Stand* and *The Happ*
Unicorns (Sidgwick & Jackson, 1971). Winner of Pernod National Youn
Poets' Competition (1971); recipient of a Gregory Award (1973).

WILLIAM PLOMER, who died last year, was born of Englis
parents in South Africa in 1903. He was educated at Rugby, then returne
to South Africa, where he worked as a farmer in the Stormberg Mountain
and as a trader in Zululand. In his early twenties he lived in Japan fo
more than two years. He wrote ten volumes of poetry, his most recen
being *Celebrations* (1972). His *Collected Poems* appeared in 1960. In 196
he was awarded the Queen's Gold Medal for Poetry. He also wrot
novels, short stories, biographies, two volumes of autobiography an
four libretti for Benjamin Britten. He was President of the Kilvert Societ
from 1968 to 1973, edited *Kievert's Dairy*. From 1968 to 1972 he wa
President of the Poetry Society.

PETER PORTER was born in 1929 in Brisbane, Australia, and
brought up in that sub-tropical city. He was educated at local public
schools and has had various jobs—newspaper reporter, warehouseman
clerk, bookseller's assistant and advertising writer. He now lives in Lon-
don and works as a freelance writer. His books of poems include *Once*
Bitten, Twice Bitten (1961), *Poems Ancient and Modern* (1964), *A Porte*
Folio (1969) and *The Last of England* (1970). *Preaching to the Converted*
and *After Martial* were published in 1972.

TULLY POTTER was born in 1942 in Edinburgh, but lived in
South Africa from 1948 to 1966 and was greatly influenced by what he
saw there. For the last eight years he has lived in Essex, where he works as
a journalist on a daily paper. He has been widely published in poetry mag-
azines in Britain and abroad; and since 1969 has run *Poetry One*, the
workshop group based in Havering.

PETER REDGROVE is widely published and anthologised, and
teaches at the Falmouth School of Art. His seven books of verse include
Dr. Faust's Sea-Spiral Spirit (Routledge, 1972) and *The Hermaphrodite*
Album (with Penelope Shuttle: Fuller D'Arch Smith, 1973). He has also
published a poem-novel called *In the Country of the Skin* (Routledge),
which won the Guardian Fiction Prize for 1973. He is represented in
Penguin Modern Poets XI and was co-editor of *New Poems 1967*. He read

cience at Cambridge, and later worked as a scientific journalist. He has ontributed to major S.F. anthologies, was Gregory Fellow in Poetry at Leeds University for three years and visiting poet to Buffalo University or one year, has travelled, lectured and taught extensively in the U.S., nd has just been appointed Visiting Professor of English at Colgate University, New York for 1974–5. Forthcoming books include *The Terrors of Dr. Treviles* with Penelope Shuttle (due from Routledge autumn 1974) nd *The Glass Cottage*, a poem-novel.

VERNON SCANNELL was born in 1922. Freelance writer. Most ecent publications: *The Tiger and The Rose*, an autobiography (Hamish Hamilton), *Selected Poems* (Allison & Busby) and *The Winter Man*, a new ollection of poems (Allison & Busby), *The Apple Road:* poems for children (Chatto & Windus).

MICHAEL SCHMIDT was born in Mexico in 1947. He studied t Harvard and Oxford, and is now Gulbenkian Fellow of Poetry at the Manchester Poetry Centre. He is Managing Director of the Carcanet Press Ltd. and, with C.B. Cox, editor of *Poetry Nation*. He has published wo books of poems, *Bedlam & The Oakwood* and *Desert of the Lions*, and edited *British Poetry since 1960: a critical survey*. His translations from he Aztec, with Ed Kissam, are projected for publication in 1974.

PENELOPE SHUTTLE was born in 1947. Her first novel, *An Excusable Vengeance*, was published by Calder & Boyars in 1967 in their volume *New Writers 6*. A second novel, *All The Usual Hours of Sleeping*, appeared in 1969. Another novel, *Wailing Monkey Embracing A Tree*, has ust been published (Calder & Boyars, London, January 1974), as have he following collections of poetry: *Photographs of Persephone* (Quarto Press), *Autumn Piano* (Rondo Publications), *The Songbook of the Snow* (a holograph collection, from Janus Press) and *The Orchard Upstairs* (The Aquila Publishing Co.). She was awarded an Arts Council Grant in 1969 and in 1972. She lives in Cornwall. Forthcoming books include *The Terrors of Dr. Treviles* (Routledge & Kegan Paul, 1974).

ALAN SILLITOE was born at Nottingham on 4 March 1928. Self-educated after the age of fourteen. Worked in factories in Nottingham. Wireless operator in air force for three years. Began writing at twenty, published at thirty with *Saturday Night and Sunday Morning* (novel, 1958). During that time lived mostly in France and Spain. Has published three volumes of poetry: *The Rats and Other Poems* (1960), *A Falling Out of Love and Other Poems* (1964) and *Love in the Environs of Voronezh and Other poems* (1968). At present getting together another book of poems. Recent fiction publications include *Raw Material* (novel, 1972); and a volume of stories, *Men Women and Children* (1973).

C. H. SISSON, was born in Bristol, 1914, and educated at the University of Bristol and in France and Germany. Wasted many years in the Civil Service and a few in the army. He now lives in Somerset, and has written novels, critical works, translations and a book on public administration, as well as the followong volumes of verse: *The London Zo* (Abelard-Schuman, 1961); *Numbers* (Methuen, 1965); *Metamorphose* (Methuen, 1968). *In the Trojan Ditch* (collected poems and selected translations) to be published by Carcanet Press in 1974.

IAIN CRICHTON SMITH was borh (1928) and brought up in the island of Lewis in the Outer Hebrides. He speaks Gaelic and English and has written in both languages. His books include two English novels, one English book of short stories, a number of English poetry books, three books of poems and short stories in Gaelic, a children's book in Gaelic and two one-act plays in Gaelic. His most recent publications are *Elegies and Love Poems* (1972) and *Hamlet in Autumn*, published in 1972.

STEPHANIE SMOLINSKY lived in London until she was eighteen. She studied English Literature at Birmingham University and since graduating, has lived in Barcelona and Paris. She has now returned to settle in London and teaches in a comprehensive school. Since the age of ten she has been writing poetry and is primarily interested in trying to express complex things in a poetry that will be available to those without a literary education.

JON STALLWORTHY was born in 1935 of New Zealander parents. He was educated at Rugby, in the Royal West African Frontier Force, and at Magdalen College, Oxford, where he won the Newdigate Prize for poetry in 1958. His publications include three collections of poems: *The Apple Barrel/Selected Poems 1956–63* (1974), *Root and Branch* (1969) and *Hand in Hand* (1974); two critical books: *Between the Lines/W. B. Yeats's Poetry in the Making* (1963) and *Vision and Revision in Yeats's Last Poems* (1969); and a biography, *Wilfred Owen* (1974). He has edited *The Penguin Book of Love Poetry* (1973); with Alan Brownjohn and Seamus Heaney he edited the P.E.N. anthology *New Poems 1970–71* and with Peter France he translated *The Twelve and Other Poems by Alexander Blok* (1970). He works for the Oxford University Press.

ANNE STEVENSON, daughter of American philosopher C. L. Stevenson, was born in Cambridge, England, in 1933. She was educated in the United States but has spent most of her life working as a teacher, a mother and a writer in Britain. Her first collection of poems was published by the University of Michigan where she was for some time a student of Donald Hall. In 1965 Twayne publishers in New York brought out her study of Elizabeth Bishop, and in 1969 a second collection of poems, *Reversals*, was published by Wesleyan University Press. Miss Stevenson is currently writer in residence at Dundee University. Her poems have appeared in the *Scotsman*, *Lines Review*, *Encounter*, *The Listener*, *London Magazine*, *Wave* and *Outposts*. Two new collections, *Travelling Behind Glass* and *Correspondences* (from which both poems printed here are taken) are forthcoming from Oxford University Press in 1974.

R. S. THOMAS was born in Cardiff in 1913. He is now Vicar of Aberdaron.

ANTHONY THWAITE was born in 1930. He has taught in universities in Japan and Libya, worked as a B.B.C. producer, was literary editor of *The Listener* and later of the *New Statesman*, and is now co-editor of *Encounter*. He has published five books of poems, most recently *New Confessions* (Oxford University Press, 1974), and a selection in the Penguin Modern Poets series.

CHARLES TOMLINSON's latest collection of verse is *Written on Water* (Oxford University Press). *Renga*, a translation into English of a composite poem by Octavia Paz, Jacques Roubaud, Edoardo Sanguineti and Tomlinson, will appear from Penguin in 1975. An exhibition of paintings, drawings and collages was held in 1972 at Oxford University Press. The poem in this anthology is the title poem of a new volume, *The Way In*, which will be appearing in the autumn of 1974.

JOHN TRIPP was born in 1927 in Bargoed, Glamorgan. He worked as a sub-editor in the B.B.C. News Division, London; as Press Officer at the Indonesian Embassy; and Information Officer in the Central Office of Information. He returned to Wales in 1968 to work as a full-time freelance writer and journalist. He has published five volumes of poetry: *The Loss of Ancestry*, *Diesel to Yesterday*, *The Province of Belief*, *Bute Park* and *The Inheritance File*. A selection of his work will soon be included in Penguin Modern Poets. He is literary editor of the magazine *Planet*, and a regular contributor to arts programmes on Harlech TV.

W. PRICE TURNER was born in York in 1927. He was Gregory Fellow in Poetry at Leeds University from 1960 to 1962, and won a Scottish Arts Council award for his collection, *The Moral Rocking-Horse*, in 1970. His earlier publications are *First Offence*, *The Rudiment of an Eye*, *The Flying Corset*, *Fables from Life* and *More Fables from Life*. As Bill Turner he has established an international following with six crime novels, the most recent being *Hot-Foot*. He is now Fellow in Creative Writing at the University of Glasgow.

JEFFREY WAINWRIGHT was born in 1944 and grew up in Stoke-on-Trent. From 1962–7 he was at the University of Leeds. Since then he has taught in the University of Wales at Aberystwyth, and for a year at Long Island University in Brooklyn, New York. He is married with two children and now lives in Manchester where he teaches in the English and History Department of the Polytechnic. His poems, and a few articles, have appeared mainly in *Stand*. A pamphlet of poems, *The Important Man*, was published by Northern House in 1970.

ANDREW WATERMAN was born in 1940 in London. After working at various clerical and manual jobs, he went to Leicester University to read English, on to Oxford to do research, and to Ireland in 1968 to take up his present post of Lecturer in English at the New University of Ulster. Since then, he has written poems that have appeared in many periodicals and been broadcast. His first collection, *Living Room*, is being published by the Marvell Press.

JANE WILSON was born in Hampshire and educated at Abbots Bromley and Streatham Froebel College. Now lives in Leeds. Has worked with deprived children, and taken drama in boys' Approved School. Currently teaches speech and drama at Huddersfield Technical Teachers Training College. Her husband, a lecturer in Marketing, and she, run two laundrettes which, she says, have made a valuable contribution to her education. Two sons. York Poetry pamphlet, *Hooligan Canute*, out spring 1974. Work broadcast in *Listen With Mother*, *Northern Drift*, and *The Sunday Collection*.